PEACE BE SHADOW WORK

A SHADOW WORKBOOK TO HEAL FROM YOUR PAST AND BREAK FREE FROM YOUR INNER CHILDHOOD TRAUMA

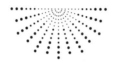

C.J. PERRY

CONTENTS

PEACE BE SHADOW WORK

A Complete Shadow Work Workbook, Guide and Journal to Heal From Your Past, Make Peace With Painful Memories and Break Free From Your Inner Childhood Trauma

A New Approach to Shadow Work

(Workbook Journal & Prompts Inside)

OR CLAIM YOURS AT
WWW.GOODSELFHEALINGHABITS.COM

A SPECIAL GIFT FOR OUR READERS

*I*ncluded with your purchase of this book is a *21 Day Deep Meditation Challenge* that will entice you to get back on track with strong meditative practices that gets you in the daily habit, creates calm in minutes and grows your knowledge to the next level as a meditator, with advanced tips and practices even if you have a busy schedule.

Click the link below and let us know which email address to send it to.

Get my FREE 21 Day Meditation Challenge

INTRODUCTION

You see, your brain as well as mine has a unique way of keeping you and I "safe." Now, I quoted the word safe because it is relative. So, what am I talking about here? Stay with me, and let's find out together.

While our bodies might be oblivious to some psychological triggers, the body, behaviors, and perceptions don't forget. Therefore, we act and feel strong unexplainable emotions pulling us out of our depths. So, you are there thinking, wondering: why? What happened? Why am I like this? Is something wrong with me? No, something isn't wrong with you. The thing is, you don't know yourself 100% as you may assume.

There are multiple shades of you. You see the brighter colors. Feel the warm hues, but what about the dark ones? Colors you can't tell. Yes, you have them. Everyone does. You, me, and that man or woman over there have one or two. They represent the fragile parts of us lost to traumatic experiences. OK, let me back up a little so you won't lose me.

These dark shades of us are from memories repressed by our brain trying to keep you and me safe. Unfortunately, we can see it is not really a safety measure we need in our lives.

New research covered by Scientific American explores the neuron circuit which the brain uses to purge harmful and hurtful memories. The findings also revealed how this particular brain activity could pose complications for treating trauma.

The brain instinctively purges memories that it deems too harmful to our mental health. It's like someone takes a part of you. Guess what? That piece is still a part of you. You might not have a vivid picture of what it looks like, or you can't even feel it, but it makes up YOU.

It's there, and you will see it come to life:

- In the kinds of decisions you make
- The friends you choose to keep
- Your sexual orientation
- What drives you
- What you do and choose not to do

…and so much more.

But here is the thing, because you don't remember the trigger or causal factor, you are unlikely to have a grip over everything I mentioned above including your decisions or motivation. And all of these play a role in your happiness. Imagine that. You leave a huge part of your sense of purpose, fulfillment, and joy to an unknown memory. You can only control what you can find solutions to of the problems you understand.

Let me paint a picture for you:

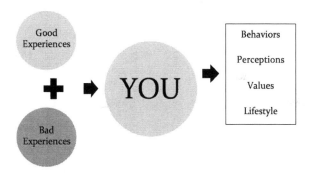

You see, both experiences make up you, which are reflected in your behaviors, perceptions, values, and the way you live your life. Yet, a huge part of what influences all of these is obscure to you.

Yes, I understand; it is best for these memories to stay purged. The experiences they reveal might crumble you right now. The past should remain in the past, right? But here is something I know, the past, especially one filled with traumatic experiences, shapes the present and predicts the future. It is not something that you shed off like a snake sheds its skin. This is reality.

Here is something else I also know and currently stand by when it comes to why we can't let go of the past, consciously, and subconsciously; that is, we can heal from it. We can be free from the pain that memory reveals and go on to live the best of our lives. And this can also be a reality. Choose this reality.

Shadow work, a form of psychoanalysis, is a technique we can use to reveal these memories or the unknown shades of us. The idea of shadow work is aimed at transforming an entity known as the "shadow" (emotional suffering or repressed memories) through self-awareness. That's right; shadow work doesn't only help reveal your shadow but transform it from a fragile being to something so much more. With shadow work, you combine your subconscious psyche and consciousness, giving your shadow the platform to reveal itself.

Now, do you know what is more fascinating than

unveiling your subconsciousness or shadow? You get to discover other parts of you that will further help you develop as a person.

It's like reading a book with a couple of its pages missing compared to a book with its pages intact. So, which tells you the whole story? Better, which of these would you prefer your life to be?

This is where this book comes in. In addition to helping you understand shadow work and implementing its techniques, you will also find out more reasons why you need to do it in the first place. I know, firsthand, that despite the appeal, you will want your shadow to stay hidden.

I mean, this is a part of us that our brain hid from reality in the first place, why unveil it? Your brain, as well as mine, were trying to protect you and I by hiding this memory. Why? Really, why should you unveil it? Yes, it helps you know all of you. But is it worth it? You must be wondering.

Get this; I completely understand. I will tell you right now that you will have doubts about this process like I did, and it is OK. It wasn't supposed to be easy, but hey, nothing good ever comes easy, right?

The idea of this book is to use shadow work to explore and heal painful memories. Thereby restoring that care-free inner child in us who is entirely free of overwhelming negative emotions that dictate our happiness.

Helping you have control over your life is why I began writing this book in the first place. I have seen first-hand what a lack of control can do. I would wake up some mornings feeling ashamed for whatever I said or did the night before. This was me. I knew it, but I didn't understand why. Stumbling upon shadow work helped me understand the why. With years of practice, I know myself better. And the positive feeling that comes with this is unmatched.

Together, you and I will go through the complete step-by-step guide from beginning to end, so you learn how to own your shadow. You will understand your shadow in a light never thought of before. Heal your past, your inner child trauma, and everything that bothers you in between. After you've learned all that you need to know about shadow work, the second part of this book is a 5-week plan that will help you implement all the knowledge you've amassed so far. With each week, you will see that hidden part of yourself come into the open. You will feel the urge to stop the process but, I know that you are 100x more powerful than your shadow (technically, it is part of you). You should be this too. So, keep at it until the very end. Do Not quit. At the end of this book, you will be able to let go and refine your life in a completely new way. Just trust the process.

So, what do you say? How much do you want this? How much do you want to know all of YOU? Every single tiny bit of it? The smiles and the frowns? The tears and the laughter? How much do you want it all?

I will prove to you that you are stronger than you may assume. So, buckle up, and let's get started!

PART I
LEARN THE SECRETS OF THE MIND

1
THE TRUTH ABOUT YOUR
DISGUSTING SIDE

*W*e have established that we all have our unpleasant sides. Therefore, no need to feel guilty or alone. You aren't alone in this journey. Together, you and I, let's reveal your darker sides. The part of you we could call "the disgusting side."

FIRST, I need you to take a slow, deep breath. Exhale. Repeat twice. Ponder. Immerse yourself in what your expectations are in this journey, and what your goals would be having achieved your expectations.

Take a minute before proceeding and truly ask yourself this question. Go ahead, this book isn't going anywhere.

WHO ARE YOU?

Have you ever sat down to wonder who you truly are? Perhaps, in some moment of silence you might have attempted to reflect upon a bad decision, a costly mistake, or a regrettable choice of words. You might think, are you different from everyone else? Why are those mistakes repeating themselves? Why does it feel like I'm stuck? The guilt from the impulses you can't control.

The guilt that stems from those moments of fragility when it seems you have no control. If ever you have been there – many of us have – then you're beginning to find yourself. You are beginning to know you. Your path to personal growth and living your life to the fullest will start from here – knowing who you are.

LET'S continue with an honest statement: you also consist of an ugly part. It is part of who you are, and if you're indeed serious about living your life to the fullest and becoming a better person, you will be open to meeting this dark, unpleasant part of you. Try this simple exercise before you and I go further.

- With a pencil, write down some negative

things about you that you're only recently coming to realize. Don't worry about how many you'll have to write. Just write.

- Write down some unpleasant things about you which you have known for long but have struggled to deal with till now. Write as many as you can.

- Look at what you have written above and reflect upon them for at least 2 minutes.

DID YOU? If so, well done.

WHILE DISCUSSING how we can embrace our inner darkness, Mateo Sol writes that "these ugly and frightening parts of ourselves are elements of the shadow self: the darker side of our nature." Therefore, you must be aware of your shadow self. It is part of who you are. That part is where many of the traumas you go through emanate from. It's like a specter, lurking, waiting, and ready to take advantage of the fissures we leave for it to pass through and show its face again.

. . .

ALSO, to learn more about who you are, look at what psychologist Carl Jung says about the shadow self. First, he emphasized that "our unconscious minds are fragmented into selves." These selves are divided into parts, based on a model he came up with called the Archetype model. These parts of you are responsible for organizing your experiences in life. Two of the major archetypes you should be aware of are your persona and shadow self. Let's find out briefly who your personal self is. The persona can be seen as your mask. The part of you that you love to show others. Simply put, who you want people to see you as. In contrast, the Shadow self is the real you. Let's get to that now.

YOUR SHADOW SELF

Let's take a gentle walk through your shadow.

First, you must be aware of your shadow. What is this shadow self? Sol writes that the shadow self "is an archetype that forms part of the unconscious mind and is composed of repressed ideas, instincts, weaknesses, desires, perversions, and embarrassment." Sheri Jacobson writes that "The shadow is the side of your personality that contains all the parts of yourself that you don't want to admit having." Let me add that it is that unconscious part of you that you can only recognize through self-awareness and effort.

Now, try to look at what you jotted down earlier on about yourself. Do they reflect your shadow self?

We are getting there.

Let me also help you with another honest statement: your shadow self isn't always negative. It is based on your perception of what you feel is dark and frail about yourself. It is this perception that may have led you to repress them. Jacobson (2017) believes that all of these depend on your perception of life and your level of self-esteem. But one thing you must understand is that everyone has a shadow. Even the nicest guy or gal on the block; or the most vivacious lady in town has a shadow.

Let's make a biblical allusion. You're Adam, and I'm Eve. Or you may reverse the role. We were born pure without any knowledge of evil, just good. We can't separate both. But as we begin to experience life, as we start to grow, we begin to feed on the tree of knowledge of both good and evil. We become aware. Our shadows are eventually born.

What did you get from this anecdote?

Think about it this way. As an infant, you are born pure. Therefore, your knowledge of life is pure and just good. However, as you start to grow and have certain experiences, you learn to separate what is good from evil. It is at this point that your shadow is born.

Sol, writing about the Persona and the Shadow, says, "The creation of the inauthentic but socially acceptable Persona birthed the creation of the authentic but damnable Shadow. Both are inseparable."

Can you differentiate your persona from your shadow self? If you're lost, just take another cursory look at the items you jotted down earlier on about yourself.

Now, let's learn about these disgusting parts of you.

THE DIFFERENT SHADOWS YOU MIGHT ENCOUNTER ON YOUR JOURNEY

The Egotistical Shadow

This is one shadow you might struggle to accept, but it is there in most people. Some of its common traits are arrogance, self-obsession, solipsism, narcissism, selfishness, self-indulgence, pomposity, etc. Are you familiar with any of these traits?

WELL, don't feel judged.

The primal cause of this shadow can be from a long period of living and feeling not good enough and "not existing, being a nobody," as Mateo Sol puts it.

Like every other shadow trait, this shadow trait starts from an experience. You certainly weren't born with it. However, let's see if you can relate to this shadow type, try this exercise:

1. Think of one time in your life someone laughed off something you did. It could be a piece you wrote, a picture you took, a grade you scored after a test, or anything else.

2. Think of one time you failed a job

interview, couldn't succeed in a competition or lost to an opponent. Perhaps it was your first defeat after many winning streaks; perhaps it was just one of many other countless other failures you have had to deal with. So how did you try to rise?

3. Think of the one time someone said something to you that severely bruised your ego. How did you react? Did you try to repress the feeling after that?

WELL, done. That is the ego side speaking.

THE NEUROTIC SHADOW

THIS PART of yourself is often caused by fear of life, others, and self. Another is a desire to regain control. As a result, you could become abnormally sensitive, obsessive, and anxious.

Some traits you might show here are paranoia, obsessiveness, impulsive suspiciousness, finicky, demanding, masochistic, compulsive, fussy behavior.

If you feel connected to this shadow type, try these exercises:

1. First, think of one trauma in your life that made you begin to question why you trusted someone.
2. Was there a time you trusted people? Think about that time and what it meant to you.
3. How did you handle your first or second betrayal if you have experienced one? Ponder about this for a moment before you read on.

THE UNTRUSTWORTHY SHADOW

THIS PART of you results from a fear of life. Yes, the fear of life.

As someone with this shadow, the traits you will show include being secretive, impulsive, frivolous, irresponsible, deceitful and/ or unreliable.

. . .

You may ask yourself, "where did this come from? Where did I first get it wrong? What was the first seed?" One could look at this type of shadow self as also coming from a background of often being distrusted as a child. Or, you grew up amongst dishonest folks whose only means of navigating through difficult situations was deception or trickery.

No, don't suppress this. Let it flow.

The Emotionally Unstable **Shadow**

This shadow emanates from a strong feeling that you can't be loved. Unresolved emotional pain can also create this shadow. It can make you feel so powerless and loathsome toward yourself.

The traits you will notice are a deep feeling of melancholia, moodiness, melodrama, manipulative, weepy, over-emotional, impulsive, and changeable.

Can you relate to these shadow traits? One experience you'd most likely have had is bullying as a child. Another could be abuse of any kind, mental or physical. Perhaps, your first reaction to these experiences brought even more abuse and loathed from the people you expected to be there for you. And, as you grew older, even as these experiences ceased from happening, your subconscious self-retained this piece of information. More so, at the slightest trigger, it shows itself in the way you respond to a partner, a friend, and in the way you approach the world.

I understand. Let's walk you through more of these parts of you.

The Controlling Shadow

THIS SHADOW IS CAUSED by the mistrust you have towards life. Other causes are the feelings of being rejected or abandoned by others around you. Another is the feeling of not being good enough.

SOME OF THE traits include being suspicious, jealousy, possessive, bossy, obsessive.

LET'S try a little exercise here. Write down each of these traits on a sheet of paper and then attach a real action of yours in the past that portrays each of the traits listed above. You may use the personal pronoun "I."

THE CYNICAL SHADOW

THE ROOT CAUSE of this shadow is the obsessive desire to protect yourself from feeling too vulnerable.

SOME TRAITS you will display are negativity, overcritical, patronizing, resentful, cantankerous, surliness.

THE WRATHFUL SHADOW

THIS COMES from a fear of others, mistrust of life, and a closed heart.

WHEN YOU HAVE THIS SHADOW, you will notice the following characteristics: ruthless, vengeful, contentious, bitchy, quick-tempered, quarrelsome, and bellicose.

Is this familiar? Don't worry; there's more.

THE RIGID SHADOW

THE ROOT CAUSE of this is "the fear and rejection of the unknown, chaos, and ego death."

WHEN YOU HAVE THIS SHADOW, you will display the following characteristics: uptight, intolerant, racist, sexist, homophobic, obstinate, uncompromising, inflexible, and narrow-minded.

THE GLIB SHADOW

THIS SHADOW SELF is caused by a distrust of life and others.

SOME OF THE traits you will display are superficiality, cunningness, inconsistency, slyness, and craftiness.

The Nonchalant Shadow

THIS IS CAUSED by grief you chose to bury, some unmitigated fear, and shame.

AS A RESULT, you become emotionally detached, distant, indifferent, uncaring, and unexciting.

The Perverted Shadow

IF YOU HAVE HAD unresolved childhood wounds, you probably have this shadow. You might also have repressed sexual desires.

THE TRAITS ARE SADISM, depravity, lust, and corruption.

The Naive Shadow

. . .

WHEN YOU REFUSE TO GROW, and when you lack the individual ego, you could develop a cowardly shadow.

Are you lost? Let's learn briefly about the individual ego.

TO UNDERSTAND THE INDIVIDUAL EGO, let's look at this quote by Philosopher Teilhard de Chardin, "We are not human beings having a spiritual experience. We are spiritual beings having a human experience."

You will grow, whether, in a good way or a negative way, you will grow. And, it is both experiences that Chardin refers to.

NOW, about the individual ego.

Well, Mateo Sol (2021), quoting psychologist, Carl Jung, defined the individuated ego as "a slow, imperceptible process of psychic growth that gradually results in a wider and more mature personality."

So, let me get you back on track.

SOME CHARACTERISTICS you will display when you have this shadow include being puerile, petty, immature, illogical, simpleminded, and vacuous.

. . .

THE COWARDLY SHADOW

THIS SHADOW SELF is caused by fear and disbelief in oneself.

WHEN YOU HAVE this shadow self, you may become weak-willed, timid, and fearful.

THE RELIER SHADOW

THIS IS another manifestation of the Shadow self. It comes from a position of always feeling vulnerable. You tend to feel a somewhat maniacal desire to be with others, take from others, or be cared for by others. As a relier, you're more comfortable depending on others than others depending on you. Do you show consistency with eliciting help from others? Even when you know, you could try and do things yourself?

People with this shadow are also believed to find

it hard trusting themselves enough to love others: they feel incapable of loving sufficiently.

SOME TRAITS A RELIER might display include obsession, pettiness, vulnerability, lack of self-love.

THE MESSIAH COMPLEX Shadow

THIS TYPE of shadow self was described by Shadow expert Jack Othon. She referred to people with this Shadow self as "people who think they're enlightened" and "can do no wrong." Whatever they do, they see it as an effort to save others. This attitude is an example of spiritual bypassing.

People with this shadow type display similar traits to the egotistical shadow. Arrogance, self-obsession, self-righteous, etc.

TAKE a three-minute break and reflect on these Shadow selves highlighted above.

Now, let's keep up.

. . .

CARL JUNG WROTE:

> "How can I be substantial if I do not cast a shadow? I must have a dark side also if I must be whole."

TAKE another minute to reflect on this quote.

WE ALL HAVE A SHADOW. Something that threatens us. Something that started this may have been when we first walked into the classroom, and every kid laughed at us. Perhaps we may have experienced our first painful rejection from someone we were in love with. Or, maybe it was our first heartbreak, an abusive parent, a bully, a loss.

Don't feel alone. Don't suppress it. That would be lying to yourself and continuing the cycle of falsehood that controls your actions and inevitably leads to more traumatic experiences.

LET'S look at this quote from Carl Jung's (1980) Psychology and Alchemy:

> "There is no light without shadow and no psychic wholeness without imperfection."

Don't be ashamed. You're not alone. It is the innate acknowledgment and awareness of this fact that makes us thick.

YOU AND YOUR SHADOW

Don't Suppress Your Shadow. Embrace it.

LOOK at this interesting line by Aletheia Luna:

> "Own your shadow, and you will own your life."

Please, don't suppress your shadow; acknowledge it. Suppressing your shadow is akin to rejecting it. And as S. Wolf puts it, "the soul feels dry, brittle, like an empty vessel" when you suppress your shadow self.

You might ask, "How can I embrace my shadow self?" That's a good question. You need to know this: don't nurture any desire that might arise in you. Embracing your shadow self doesn't mean basking in the negative or indulging it. For instance, when

31

you indulge hate or pride, it will only result in more hate and pride.

THEREFORE, to untether your mind, it's important to acknowledge the existence of these things. The result is that you will begin to walk through the uncharted paths within your soul. You'll then realize that you are not these demons, but they are just elements you picked up as you progressed in your life's journey.

So, what does it mean to embrace your shadow self? It means you can accept it. You shouldn't live in denial of its existence anymore. You can't defeat pride if you're still struggling to accept that you're proud.

HOW CAN you experience self-love if you don't accept your lack of it? As Mateo Sol puts it,

66 "we must learn to face our Shadow Selves honestly, and voyage into the dark, murky waters of the unknown courageously. Otherwise, every time we condemn other people for their shadow traits, we're in essence

condemning our hypocritical selves in the process."

Here are a few things to note in your journey to acceptance.

- Be truthful; be honest.
- Have courage.
- Reconcile all your parts; attain inner unification.

Come to think of it, are you aware that there are amazing qualities hidden in your shadow? Many of these qualities stay hidden even as you suppress your shadow self. As a result, you might have suppressed that artistic part of you, that innovative part of you, or that creative part.

SELF-EXPRESSION IS KEY TO SHADOW DISCOVERY

One way to express yourself is to write and to paint. There's always an element of oneself in the things he or she writes. The characters a writer creates in a book can embody some characteristics of their own shadow. At that moment, the writer has brought their shadow to life through their characters. That way, they can learn more about their own inner darkness; they can learn about their caprices.

There is an unconscious revelation of your inner hidden person as you write, as you tell a story. Similarly, the painter finds himself in his art. He engages in the purgation of the deepest sentiments and emotions no other experience can unearth.

HERE'S AN EXERCISE FOR YOU: ponder upon what interest or skill, such as those mentioned above, that can help you discover and embrace your shadow.

IF YOU HAVEN'T MET your shadow self yet, Don't worry, you'll find it.

WELL, how do you feel right now? Are there things worth reflecting on from what you have read in this chapter? Your path to personal growth is very much promising, so stay focused. You might want to take a short break before moving into the next chapter, it is where you will be able to explore the mind of the shadow, or should I say its consciousness.

2
INTO THE SHADOW'S
CONSCIOUSNESS

*H*ello there. You've made significant progress in your journey to self-discovery and healing. You'll have to encourage yourself at this juncture because you've been splendid. Take a brief look at your notes from the previous chapter. If you haven't taken any notes, I strongly encourage you to re-read the chapter and do so if you truly want this to work for you. If you still want to move forward, then what is strongly recommended is taking notes for the rest of the chapters because it is about to get heavy. Write all over this book if you must.

Now, you'd have realized how we are transitioning into the cognitive state of your Shadow self; that is, your shadow consciousness.

.   .   .

IN THIS CHAPTER, I'll try to help you become more aware of your shadow self. I'll take delicate steps as you and I begin this aspect of your journey. Our goal, together, will be to help you explore the mind of your shadow. In addition to this, you'll get to know about your past, inner lost child, and accept what it was and what it has become. You know why we must do this? Because you can't win if you don't know your enemy. So, let's begin by finding out who this enemy is as we explore the shadow consciousness.

THE SHADOW: THE YOU IN YOU

Imagine yourself as a child; let's say, an 8-year-old boy or girl. The world seems to be turned against you. You're the only child of a mother who was raped before you were conceived. Neither you nor your mom knows the whereabouts of your dad, and your mom, because of the shame from the world around her, abandons you in the arms of a hostile family, far away. For every mistake you make, this family reminds you that you're a bastard whose parents abandoned them.

At school, you feel like a misfit, especially because your schoolmates would tease and bully you; they see you as dumb and ugly. When you return home again, you're bullied and abused by the people you live with. You begin to feel even more alone. You spend most time alone at the corner, a spot you chose for yourself to squat and mope.

Sometimes, you sit there, folding your arms and legs and talking to an invisible friend or imagining happy imaginations as a way of escaping the reality that embraces you. As you grow older, you become distant, melancholic, and believing you're unlovable, but yet seeking to be loved. You become a complex emotional wreck or something worse or different, but just as bad. And, like your child-self, you suppress your experiences by getting lost in a manic reverie filled with fantasies or fancy imaginations.

TAKE a little while to think about the above scenario. Did you connect with it? Of course, not to a point where your experiences are the same, but to a point where there is a sync in the pain you've felt before and the one described above.

Now, try to connect this with the point we made in chapter one, where we mentioned that we're all born pure. We came with just good thoughts – pure beings – but as we start to grow older and experience life, we begin to eat from the tree of the knowledge of good and evil. We can now separate good from evil as we begin to experience both.

So, again, what's the shadow? Writer and professional coach, Scott Jeffrey defined the shadow as

> "the 'dark side' of our personality because it consists chiefly of primitive, negative human emotions and impulses like rage, envy, greed, selfishness, desire, and the striving for power."

Can you connect this definition with the experiences of the 8-year-old child described above?

LET'S DO THIS: from the lesson in chapter 1 of this text, try to identify what you feel may constitute the shadows of this 8-year-old child. You may also do this by connecting the child's bad experiences with the definition of a shadow you read in chapter one.

Now, let's add to the above information. Your shadow also constitutes the part of you that doesn't correspond to the sort of image you want to portray of yourself. Often, you end up burying it except that it doesn't stay buried. It lives to control your actions albeit unknowingly.

Your shadow is part of your unconscious being. Did you notice the use of the words "unconscious" and "being?" What does this mean to you? Well, you can think of something unconscious as something that isn't awake, or that isn't aware. Now, what is a being? Well, a being is something that exists, and it may be conscious or not , yet it exists, temporarily.

Are you lost here? OK. Look at it this way. Your shadow is unconscious because you made it to be, but it's still part of your being, and, like every being, it doesn't stay unconscious forever. It can be awakened or triggered by deliberate or calculated action. Your shadow is that part of you that is unsuitable for the conscious part of you and as a result, you relegate it to your dark side.

Try this exercise:

- Set aside a sheet of white paper.
- With a pencil, write anything you can think of on the paper.
- Try to erase what you've written by shading over the words you wrote.
- Look at the paper again.
- Observe for traces of what you've written before.

At the end of the exercise you just did above, what did you notice? Well, this is what you might have noticed:

1. Even after shading over the items you wrote, you might still see traces of what you wrote, and
2. The once-white sheet of paper is now filled with smears as a result of attempting to erase what you have written through shading.

BE STILL, take a deep breath, there's more. Because the goal is to fully explore the mind of your shadow and fully understand all that there is to possibly know about your past, inner lost child, and accept what it is, let's see how else we can understand the shadow before we go into its consciousness.

Have you heard of analytical psychology? Yes, we mentioned a bit of that in chapter one; however, let's talk a little bit about it.

SOME PEOPLE CALL it the Jungian analysis. Well, it's a term coined by Swiss psychiatrist, Carl Jung. He used this term to describe research on his study of the psyche.

Why are you getting to know a little bit about him? Yeah, this is it: in his field of analytical psychology, he found out that your shadow can be either the part or aspect of your personality that isn't conscious or that your "conscious ego" doesn't identify with. Let's also say that it is all the parts of you that you aren't fully conscious of; that is, your unknown side as we discussed in chapter one.

Also, this shadow mind is sort of like the Freudian unconscious. Let me explain. The Freudian unconscious is a concept developed by Austrian psychoanalyst, psychologist, and neurologist Sigmund Freud. This unconscious mind includes your thought processes, motivations, and interests.

These processes happen automatically in your subconscious mind. You can't examine them as they occur because you probably aren't aware of them.

YOUR UNCONSCIOUS PART INCLUDES:

- Feelings you have repressed,
- Fears and desires you might have hidden,
- Automatic skills,
- Extreme perceptions,
- Automatic reactions, and
- Complexes

Well, you can see how these two psychologists are able to create parallels to what we are discussing here in this chapter: the shadow consciousness. Now, try to connect the activity you did earlier on with your knowledge of the shadow mind, repressed feelings, and the unconscious mind. What's the similarity? Yes, your shadow is like a smear, the more you try to cover it the more unpleasant (untidy) it becomes.

Let's move on. Do you know how the shadow thinks? You probably have some ideas about this as a result of what you have learned in chapter one and what we have done so far in this chapter. But let's still talk about it.

HOW THE SHADOW THINKS

You now know what the shadow is, so it's time to learn something more: how it thinks. By understanding how your shadow thinks, you'll further enhance your path to victory and getting the best out of yourself. But remember this as you learn about how the shadow thinks: you can't be afraid of your shadow because it is part of who you are, and you can't be afraid of yourself. Embrace you!

LET'S BEGIN WITH THIS. Your shadow is a being; we have established that. Your shadow speaks and acts spontaneously. It has a voice. You have often said things that portray a certain personality trait you may have one day argued that it never existed inside of you. Many of us have. For instance, we may have said to someone, "Oh, I'm not a bigot." Or "I'm not proud or hateful." However, sometimes, we subconsciously say or do things that portray the opposite of what we project to people. That's your shadow voice speaking in this instance.

> *Remember this: The thoughts that flow from your shadow are, let's say, unlimited.*

Shadow expert, Jordan Grey, once held a group session with some people who wanted to understand themselves more, and during that session, he listened to them say a lot of things that portrayed what your shadow, my shadow, really thinks. I will list some of them below.

"I think I'm better than most people."

"I THINK I'm worse than most people."

"I HATE men for ruining the world."

"I THINK that women truly are the inferior sex. They say they don't need men, but I feel like they would flounder on their own and they're afraid of how much they need us."

"MY PAIN IS MORE significant than the pain of others."

· · ·

"I WISH that there were wolves in the streets who would feast on the weakest people in my community. It would strengthen the gene pool and get rid of all of the talentless losers."

"I SHOULD HAVE MORE money than 99.9% of the world because I will do better things with it than most people would."

"I THINK that people (over the age of 25) who accept minimum wage jobs have low self-esteem and deserve the societal position they have opted themselves into."

"I LOVE the feeling of being completely in control of someone sexually. It makes me feel powerful."

"I LOVE MANIPULATING men into giving me what I want."

"I WISH that my mom had died instead of my dad."

. . .

"I WISH that the bottom stupidest person of the world would just disappear. Or at least that it would be made illegal for people under a certain IQ to procreate."

"SOMETIMES I HATE women for how much power their sexual energy has over me.

"I LOVE the idea that I could coast through my entire life on my looks, my body and my charm alone."

WELL, intriguing right? These are just a few of the examples provided, but you'll find that these thoughts represent one, two, or more of the things we've said or thought of at one point in time.

YOU ARE WHAT YOU THINK ABOUT

Look at the statement above. Have you heard that before? What do you think about it? Is it true? See it this way. When you eat pasta prepared by an Italian and pasta prepared by let's say, a German, there should be a difference, right? Of course. Except they both learned to cook pasta from the same people.

Now, why'd their pasta taste different? It's because of the ingredients (or content) in the food. Therefore, we judged both meals (even though they're both kinds of pasta) based on their contents. You aren't who you are because of your looks, but because of what you think both inwardly and outwardly. Let's stay on track now.

Come to think of it. Would you say any of the things listed above before a large crowd in a graduation ceremony? Would you say any of them in a church or other social gathering? Probably not. Why? Because you wouldn't want to project a certain image. Think about it! Also, do you know that even if you don't believe or accept a thought you have, it could still be your legitimate shadow image? Surprising, right?

Now, take a deep breath, and like you've been doing so far, try to reflect on some things you have said before that perhaps contradict the image people have about you. Here's what I'd do: I'd write them down and possibly the approximate time and occasion I said such or even had the thought. This brief exercise will help you understand your shadow better.

THE BAGGAGE WE CLAIM DOESN'T EXIST

Let's be frank, everyone has a burden – a *heavy, heavy, heavy,* burden. We know these burdens. Rents we must pay, illnesses we're treating, vices we are dealing with and are aware of, taxes we have to take care of, and the pains we are nursing: these are all part of the visible burdens we acknowledge. Nevertheless, you also bear burdens you think don't exist; we all do. Does this intrigue you? At this rate, it shouldn't. What should perhaps intrigue you is that some of these invisible burdens are heavier because they represent character flaws or weaknesses that can be costly, simply because we ignore them.

LET'S take a cursory glance at some of the quoted statements earlier. Look at this one, "I have fantasized about being raped." What character does it represent to you? OK, let's look at this other one: "I love the idea that I could coast through my entire life on my looks, my body and my charm alone." From what you discovered in chapter one about the shadow traits you might encounter, what shadow traits would either of the two fall under? Perhaps, the "perverted shadow" for the earlier and the "egotistical shadow" for the latter.

One thing you must know is this: particles in your inner parts which may come in the form of addiction (porn, drugs, alcohol, smoking, sex) represent burdens that overwhelm your will to live a more fulfilled and peaceful life. So, to be more candid, you must own this part of your life or else they will own you. *You've got to own the baggage within.* If you don't want to destroy your relationships, or ruin your career or dreams, don't take that italicized statement with a pinch of salt.

HOW CAN you discover even more of the baggage within you? Try these exercises to become more aware of the aspects of yourself that you're withholding and bring those things to light (to consciousness) healthily and responsibly.

- What biases do I hold towards the opposite sex?
- What stereotypes do I have towards people from a different race, color, or culture?
- Do I hate anyone, and to what extent?
- What are the worst things I have said in the past few days?
- Did I hurt anyone recently?

- What are my prejudices towards men?
- To what extent do I desire to be rich?
- Do I feel smarter and intellectually superior to anyone?

Take a while to think about those for a second. Perhaps write your answer. Does it direct you to certain feelings about yourself you didn't imagine existed? Did you dig up shadow thoughts or baggage you didn't know you carried before? If it did, then you're on the right path, if it didn't, don't worry.

THE SHADOW KNOWS THE REAL YOU

You may not be conscious of your shadow self, but it is conscious of you. It is aware and knows what is hidden behind your facade. The shadow knows the real you. Just the way you are aware of your being, so does the shadow.

THINK about this statement by writer, Kimberly Fosu,

66 "The shadow is an inner fragmentation that occurs within you. It's almost like

two different people are operating your life."

To add to this, your projections are often sentimental and biased. It's like a mom who has two sons but is more comfortable showing off the one who performs excellently well in their academics but hides the one who struggles in class. Are they her children? Sure. Do they know her? Certainly. Therefore, as much as you project a positive image of yourself, you can't hide "yourself" from "yourself". In clearer terms, we can't deceive ourselves.

> *The things you feel aren't suited to your preferred conscious attitudes; they are usually tossed to your dark side.* ~C.J. Perry~

THE NIGHTMARES YOUR SHADOW MAKES

Have you ever heard the term, "ghost from your past?" Well, you're that ghost from your past. I mean, the subconscious, rejected, but existing self.

LET'S PAINT A PICTURE HERE. Imagine a figure appearing at night. Clothed in all the possible darkness, this figure lurks around, unseen, invisible, but present. You can only feel its presence maybe by a gust of wind, the strange unsettling of utensils, or the swift swaying of window curtains. You're probably experiencing this mysterious occurrence for the first time being alone.

Suddenly, you see a figure in a white, blood-stained flannel appear and dash out into the darkness again, of course, your fear begins to mount. You begin to develop a sudden adrenaline rush. Then, after a big flash of lightning and a roar of thunder from outside the window strikes, the figure reappears. But this time much closer than before, and like a quick flash, you see the face of a familiar dead person from your past. You awake.

NIGHTMARES AREN'T ANYTHING PLEASANT. They aren't things you want to recall or even project. As much as some people love to read horror stories or watch them at the cinema, there aren't many who want to have such experiences in real life. They're like our nightmares, that is, those horror stories. Why don't we enjoy them when we see them in our dreams? Because they aren't experiences that we want to be associated with.

Beyond the external validation, we will lose when these shadow nightmares pop out within us, they also inflict pain within us. They fan the embers of fear, anxiety, and doubts about ourselves. All we deny in ourselves—whatever we perceive as inferior, evil, or unacceptable—become part of the shadow.

Now, remember that these nightmarish parts of you were formed from the experiences you had as life happened to you.

OBSERVE THIS: *Lola was once a happy and cheerful 11-year-old, but when her parents died in a motor accident, she experienced a sudden personality shift even she didn't anticipate. Well, it started with her moving to live with her relatives in a faraway city. Unlike her former city, the people she met in this new city were mean, daring, insensitive, uncaring and very individualistic. No one stood up for anyone or pitied another if he or she were in a difficult circumstance. She didn't know this.*

Hence, one day in school, while she was eating during lunch, one of the older boys pushed her off the bench that she was sitting on. She fell off, hurting herself a little. She looked around, hoping to get some sympathy or help; instead, everyone stared at her, laughing. Lola gets up, she looks around and feels ashamed; she walks off sobbing.

20 years later, Lola is going to stand before a crowd of college graduates to give a valedictorian speech. She graduated summa cum laude. Lola is often known to be extremely shy, reserved, and anti-social. This will be the biggest crowd she'll ever stand before.

As she begins, she also realizes that the last time she was amid a crowd as large as this, she was only 11-years old, and they laughed at her. Lola knows that for the first time, the part of her she has always suppressed could either be hidden or be used to her advantage. She could either hide from her nightmare or come out to face it. This was her moment!

HOW TO FIND THE SHADOW IN YOUR LIFE

Have you ever told someone who has been bothering you to "get lost?" Sure, we all have. Perhaps not literally and not always to an external being, but our internal subconscious self. It's time to find that guy or gal we told to get lost!

HERE ARE three things renowned shadow expert Kimberly Fosu suggested we can do to find our shadow.

. . .

Projection

We often see others as a mirror or a projection of ourselves. This is an unconscious (shadow) behavior. What happens when we do this is that we project the problems we have on others. That is, as we find something we dislike about ourselves, we sort of point it out on others.

Task: Be more attentive to how and what you project towards someone else. You'll find your shadow between the dotted lines. It's like the sort of attention you pay while looking into a mirror, but this time, the other person is your mirror.

Triggers

A gun has a lever, when pulled, it activates its firing mechanism. This lever is called a trigger. There are shells containing bullets of experiences you've had in the past that after one action of yours or someone else's, everything from before is set in motion. We begin to recall events and things we may have buried, or thought were lost years ago.

TASK: To find yourself, be attentive to your triggers. Find them so that they'll help you find your past pains and shadow self.

PATTERNS

LIKE TRIGGERS, the patterns that we observe about ourselves can point us to our shadow. It just requires you to be observant and conscious about them and you will find them. One thing you've noticed in this chapter is that we established some truths, and one of them is that your shadow can reflect itself in your outward reality. As these reflections occur consistently, you'll notice their footprints and as well their patterns.

Task: What are the most consistent reflections of your shadow that you can construct in your mind right now? Are there enough patterns to create a picture of that shadow? Take a little while to think about this.

· · ·

I HOPE you can believe in your ability to heal your past, but even that belief must be accompanied by the action steps outlined above. Look at the tasks again if you feel the need to before moving on to the next chapter where you'll learn the steps you can take to healing.

3

PUTTING THE PIECES TOGETHER

SHADOW INTEGRATION

*J*n the previous chapter, you were able to successfully enter the shadow's consciousness. You walked through the mind of your shadow as well as how your shadow thinks. For us to reflect a little bit on that before we go further, can you try to create a picture of you walking into your head? (Just the way you walk into a dark and deserted street not knowing what you'll find there) Look at this book cover. What do you see? Now, as you begin to walk further into your head, reflect on the things you can remember about the shadow's consciousness. As you reflect, try to integrate them.

How can you do this?

· · ·

CREATE a mental picture of the baggage you end up finding in that dark and solitary part of your head. Then, as you go further into the vast spaces of your head, imagine you see a person hiding in the chaos before you. They come out and bare themself, naked. You are intrigued by this sight. You feel haunted. You aren't intrigued because there's a stranger in a place you assumed to be uninhabited. You aren't even intrigued because they are naked. You're intrigued because you realize you know this person. And, it is this fact that haunts you: they are you!

So, we've helped you find your shadow self. You've discovered him along with the baggage he bears. Like a lost and found prodigal son, it's about time we learned how to integrate him. Therefore, what we'll try to do together in this chapter is to learn and understand how to work your shadow into what it is designed to do. Also, you'll learn how to use your shadow to your benefit instead of allowing it to destroy you.

Well, before you continue, take a deep breath and prepare your mind. Make every thought single and focused.

. . .

Now, let's begin.

One thing you must know is this: you must be willing and able to integrate some elements of your shadow work to achieve the best of yourself. Shadow work expert, Kylie Fuller, says that "to become your highest self, you must embrace your darkest self."

Therefore, think of yourself as a basket of cherries, oranges, and lemons. Now, imagine you want to make a nice fruit drink and all you do is use just the cherries and throw away the oranges and lemons. Wouldn't that be wasteful? However, you'd be wiser to make the best out of the whole of you by integrating them, that is, these fruits, instead of simply, "cherry-picking."

> *"The quest to become our highest self isn't about cherry-picking our best qualities and nurturing those attributes. It's about seeing yourself, the beautiful and the ugly, and learning how to be your best version of that whole."* – Kylie Fuller

> *"What is not brought to consciousness, comes to us as fate."* – Carl Jung

In the previous chapters, you were able to

explore and uncover the darkest parts of your subconscious self. At the beginning of this chapter, you tried to reflect, through an image-building exercise, on what you've uncovered in the previous chapter; that is, the person that sort of represents your subconscious mind – your shadow self. Now, after all you've known about this person, how do you integrate they? Let's continue with this exciting journey.

INTEGRATING YOUR SHADOW

Our stories are different; therefore, as you'll come to realize, your journey to finding and coming to terms with your unique shadow will be somewhat different from others. However, what's most important is that like everyone in this journey, you arrive at your destination.

Let's look at some of the key elements to integrating your shadow – making it whole with yourself.

ACCEPT that your shadow is Part of You. Accept Also, that It Doesn't Define You.

Imagine you were a coin. Of course, coins have two parts. Now, imagine you're a coin that could think, speak, walk and live like a human. One day, while you lay flat like every coin, the left side of yourself decides that it wants to go fishing, but you, being the right side, decide that you want to go to the museum. Rather than agree, you both deny each other, and you find "yourself" stuck and not making any progress.

Eventually, after being stuck for so long, you accept your other side and decide to go anywhere it wants to go, fishing, hunting, and bowling. Well, this isn't the best of you either, as you're catering to just one side of you – the left side. Eventually, you decide to have another discussion where you agree to agree eventually. You realize that you're both the same people acting differently. And, for you to progress as a whole entity, you must have one common goal: you must have one collective destination.

Therefore, as you come to terms with the other part of you, you must be ready to accept this newly acknowledged part of you. Your shadow self doesn't make you or define you, just the same way you can't judge a lion by its tail. See your shadow, as the other part of you which needs to be in sync with your other self, needs to be accepted so you can control it.

Look at it this way. Let's say you tend to feel hatred towards people. You can't just tell yourself, "Oh, well, I'm a hateful person, so I should just go on and live like that." The truth is, shadow work doesn't require you to become solely your dark side or to allow it to define your behavior or personality. It requires you to integrate your shadow self to be able to control it rather than allowing it to control you.

MAKE a Journal of Your Hidden Parts.

Life and time reveal the hidden parts of us. It's like marriage or relationships. The more you experience your partner, the more you learn about them. The same thing happens to us in life generally. We're always on a journey of self-discovery.

Therefore, you must journal your revelations as you discover hidden parts of yourself. You must write down your experiences. What are the things about yourself that you're just beginning to discover? Each day, make it a point of duty to add to your journal every new thing you find about yourself. It doesn't matter how little or great it is: write it.

What sort of challenges do you think you might face in your shadow work journey if you failed to write down your experiences? Well, every individual is different, but you can only retain new information you write down. Below is an excerpt of Kylie's written experience on the challenges he faced when he failed to document his shadow journey:

> *"I failed to write down my self-revelations early in the shadow work journey. I felt there was no point. I meditated internally on my shadow self, so why should I write about it? This poor habit came back to bite me later. I found myself rediscovering parts of my shadow I had recognized previously and forgotten about. Shadow work isn't effective if you don't remember what you find."*

Find a strategy that works for you. Remember that, when you journal the revelations about yourself, you allow yourself to explore this newly discovered side of yourself. You'll also be able to recollect the new revelations as you write them down.

To gain even more insight about journaling and picking apart your shadow, I advise you to invest into our practical journal: Peace Be Shadow: A Shadow Work Journal by C.J. Perry. You can find it on Amazon or our website at Goodselfhealinghabits.com. There you'll find deep profound questions that won't be found in this book, that are bold, daring and challenging to answer but are only for your growth.

OBSERVE YOUR RESPONSE.

It is important to pay attention to your reactions. Why do you think it's important? Well, paying attention to and observing your reactions are important to your shadow work journey because it helps you fully explore your shadow self. By doing this – exploring – you can learn more about it.

THE TRUTH IS, the best and worst of us are revealed in the most difficult, discomforting, and perhaps, unpleasant situations. If you lived with very nice, familiar, easy-going, and amazing people, it'll be difficult to know the extent to which you can be tolerant or intolerant.

But let's say for the first time, you meet a set of strangers with completely different cultural, social backgrounds or political views, how would you behave amongst them? Of course, these situations will likely reveal some aspects of you that you never anticipated. Does your behavior in a pressure situation contrast with your behavior in a familiar and less hostile situation?

The truth is our reactions are often spontaneous when we find ourselves in these hostile situations. What this means is that, under difficult situations, we don't give ourselves enough time to think before we act or respond. How do you react to the person who jumps the queue from behind to stand just in front of you? How do you react when someone throws a slur or a stereotype at you? All these situations are likely to elicit knee-jerk responses from you rather than calculated, well-thought responses.

Therefore, it is important to pay attention to these instinctive reactions of yours as they're often products of your shadow self. You can compare this to a cloth you have just washed and rinsed to dry. The tighter you squeeze; the more water flows out from the cloth.

Learn to teach yourself to monitor your reactions. Learning this doesn't happen immediately, but with more effort, belief, and commitment on your part, you'll learn it. And when you learn it, there's a great deal about your shadow you'll discover.

Don't criticize or rationalize your intuition.

As you recognize an aspect of your shadow self, you might want to analyze its existence, intellectualize it, or second guess it. It's happened to many of us, so don't feel alone here. In fact, it's difficult to avoid.

Imagine your reaction the first time you realize you have just used a word or expression that may have hurt a child badly. Or the first time you acted upon your anger and violently hit someone who upset you. You may be tempted at this point, to question this particular action of yours because it shows a different aspect of you that you never believed existed. Well, remember this: your shadow work journey isn't a journey to validation; it is a path to discovery, and recovering all you may have hidden for so long.

Ultimately, you'll come to realize that your shadow self isn't the part of you that you can have a rational conversation with. It's an aggressive part of you that has a forceful effect on you. That is why you had to repress it rather than encourage it. Therefore, as part of your integration process, don't criticize or question the existence of your shadow self.

Shadow Work is a Lifetime Process

One of the unique things about the shadow work experience is that it is not a once-in-a-lifetime experience. Do you know why? Well, it's because even when we have completed a shadow work cycle, life still hasn't ended its pages, chapters of stories, and experiences. We learned earlier on that, a lot of the darks side of us are born from certain early childhood traumas. However, some traumas happen at adult age, not just childhood. We can't guess the impact they'll have on our personality, morality, or even behavior.

Shadow work is to our mind what bathing is to our physical body. You can't say because you bathed today that you'll never bathe again, certainly not. The reason being that, as you walk around, you'll accumulate dirt on your body, and you'll need to wash it. Similarly, you'll always have experiences that may plant negative memories, or that may hurt you or push you, or even question your sanity. That's life for you.

More so, it is important to note that, integrating your shadow isn't something you can accomplish in a lifetime. So, don't be discouraged. The growth you seek requires consistency and continuity.

FOLLOW and Observe Your Assessment of Other People.

You may be wondering, "How does this help me integrate my shadow?" Well, as you've learned so far, you can't integrate a shadow if you don't even recognize or know it exists. Therefore tracking your perceptions or judgments of other people is important to find your shadow.

. . .

ALLOW me to explain this better. Do you recall what we discussed about projecting ourselves onto others? Yes, this is it. The things we project onto others are most often a reflection of ourselves. We may conclude someone is hateful or egotistical because he or she didn't agree with a religious or political view we share whereas we might just be the ones who are hateful and egotistical for not under-standing that not everyone must agree with or accept our views regarding politics and life generally.

> The aspects of our shadow that we are least in relationship with are the things we are the fastest to perceive and judge in others. – Jordan Grey

LOOK AT THIS STORY:

Lisa and Mark have been dating for about a year now. Mark is currently a college student in his 3rd year studying Psychology at Oxford University, UK, while Lisa is a college dropout who now works at a retail store in Houston. Lisa had to leave college because she could no longer cope with the stressful academic schedule; plus, she was beginning to have serious anxiety issues. Lisa and

Mark met on Facebook, but they decided to get to see each other when he came for holiday in the US a year and a half earlier. Since then, it's been almost perfect between them. But lately, Lisa has been having doubts about Mark's honesty and commitment to her. Although they speak just as often as they used to, and he still texts and calls her those lovely names, she couldn't fathom him not cheating or leaving her for someone else.

He too has noticed that her tone towards him has changed from that of trust to uncertainty. Some days back, she abruptly ended a video chat with him after she was convinced, he had been cheating. His facial expressions were unusual to her; he looked uncomfortable looking at her during the call. As a result, she interpreted his facial expression as guilt from cheating. Although Mark has often proven his commitment to her, she couldn't imagine him being committed to someone like her, a college dropout, who is often depressed and emotionally volatile.

When they speak again today, she intends to confront him further about her suspicions and to inform him that she has already cheated on him twice since they last spoke. She did this with a male friend of hers who has been making advances at her for a while now. She felt weak and encouraged by the thought that Mark would've been doing the same as his body language during the last video chat proved.

Soon, her phone rings, and Mark begins to apologize for how he behaved the last time they spoke. He explains that he failed an exam and it affected him mentally. He had been drinking and was trying to hide that from her as she has always been against him drinking. On hearing this, Lisa begins to feel bad about her actions from the last conversation.

She explained that she judged him based on her insecurities. She eventually decides to still open up to him about her cheating. She explained why she had to do it hoping he'd understand. Angry, feeling betrayed, and even more disappointed, Mark cries that he has never cheated on her with anyone. After the long emotional exchanges between them, he begins to feel even more depressed and angry and so he calls off the relationship at that moment. The two end up being severely heartbroken.

SIMPLE TASK:

- What do you think were Lisa's insecurities? You could maybe write them down mentally or on a sheet of paper.
- What character flaws of Lisa did she project on Mark?

Most times, we don't get the best out of our relationships because of an experience like that of Lisa and Mark. When we observe the things we project in others, we can discover that those flaws are ours. They are personal flaws we subconsciously assume others possess. Therefore, it is important to notice the things we criticize about others; perhaps, it might just be a personal shadow we need to understand and integrate.

Find an Intimate Relationship

You'll agree that one thing an intimate relationship does is that it brings out the best and worst of us. The moment you feel so loved by someone, it can bring a sense of unease and unworthiness inside you. Maybe you can't believe someone could even love you the way you are.

Also, we tend to draw a line of territory between us, who are in love, and an outside intruder. How do you react when you see a person making advances at your spouse? In addition, our ego junks are more manifest when we're in love.

As stated earlier, yes, you feel too comfortable with this person that you may begin to exhibit traits you never recognized before. You could become judgmental of the other, you could become petty in some situations, or you could even become irritable with your underlying character traits or responses in sensitive situations.

You must take note of these shadow selves as they spring up, but don't judge or condemn them. Do the job of integrating them by identifying them, owning them, and assimilating them.

Group Work Therapy

Group work therapy works like a mirror. You can sit in a group of two, three, or more people, while you each take turns to share your peculiarities. What you'll realize is that as you listen to one another share a part about themselves, you're also encouraged to share a lot too about yourself. More so, you'll get to see yourself even in the things they share about themselves.

It's important you participate fully in group sessions and not just be an onlooker. Showing full commitment during this process of shadow work will work wonders for you. Whether or not it's something you love doing, trying it out will yield tremendous results in the long run.

The Many Benefits of Integrating Your Shadow

- The process of integrating your shadow results in self-acceptance. Self-acceptance helps you become less critical and even more accepting of others.
- It helps you become more humble.
- More so, as you own your shadow self, it'll lead you to wholeness and balance.
- It helps bring out a sense of genuine maturity in you.
- You'll achieve peace and comfort within yourself.
- As you let go of the repression within you, there is an energy you'll release that'll improve your health.
- Oh, yes! Make your dark side your pal as it'll greatly improve creativity. Think of this expression: paint your pain!

As we round off this chapter, it's important to take time to think about many of the key points you have taken down regarding shadow integration. Remember again, commitment is key, and it is your commitment that'll lead to your consistency. Keep in mind, again, that you aren't alone. You're special in this walk and the amazing things about your life will manifest themselves in a successful journey that may be bumpy occasionally.

Keep this quote in mind as you prepare to read the next chapter.

> *"The short answer to healing and integrating our shadow is this: become aware of the parts of yourself that you are rejecting, and bring those things forward into your life healthily and responsibly"* – Jordan Grey, Shadow Expert.

PART II
WORK YOUR WAY THROUGH IT WITH A 5-WEEK PRACTICAL PLAN

4

JOURNALING IN THE SHADOWS

PRACTICE YOUR SHADOW WORK

*A*s you begin the second part of this journey, what are your expectations for yourself? Would you like to write them down? You may tailor your expectations with the contents of this part of the book. Personalize it as much as you can. You can make the most of this journey when you take deliberate steps such as this.

IN THE PREVIOUS PARTS, you learned about the shadow mind. You discovered truths about your disgusting side, and you were able to delve into the shadow consciousness. As you read further, you'll be doing more practice at this stage. The best way to build on what you have learned is to try to take practical steps that will help you overcome your trauma and get the best out of your relationships.

> "Our shadows develop primitively and instinctively as a survival mechanism, so while they may not contain attractive qualities, they're largely beyond our control and have served a vital purpose at some time. But the fact is, they can remain hidden deep within us long beyond when they stopped serving us, and this is actually a clue to identifying our own particular shadow traits" – Refined Rose

WHAT IS A SHADOW WORK JOURNAL?

A shadow journal is simply a journal that you use for your shadow work exercise. It could be a notepad or a notebook. You must keep it safe. However, you might want to share it with a therapist during a session, a friend you trust, or perhaps you'd prefer to keep every detail a secret. It's up to you.

Journaling your shadow is an important step to integrating your shadow and healing, so you'll begin this part by learning more about the gold standard for shadow work and healing – journaling.

During the journaling process, some prompts

will be provided for you. We'll be using these prompts to guide you. Now, let's look at why these prompts are important.

Why Shadow Work Prompts & Exercises Are Important

First, they are important because they can help you restore harmony. For example, journaling can be combined with other exercises such as meditation, breath work , visualizing practices and more. Besides, there's also the awesome fact that you can have what you've written on record which can be useful for reference and exploring deeper aspects of yourself.

Also, this exercise will help you to identify hurtful truths about the things you've repressed and denied. Part of the truth you'll come to appreciate is that you can only control yourself. So, rather than spend most of your energy trying to force certain behaviors on others, work on yourself instead.

Before you begin, look at the following objectives we outlined for you. At the end of this session, you should be able to:

- Get in touch with your shadow self
- Learn new information about your shadow self and
- & Integrate yourself with your shadow

Firstly, you must realize that it is unhealthy to be overwhelmed by the shadow self. Therefore, to avoid this, acknowledge that this part of you is important, and it is the reason why you are undertaking this important exercise.

Furthermore, the journaling activity will help you explore and discover your shadow side. It'll lead you to the authentic, energetic, and creative part of you. No matter what your shadow is, whether it be anger, low self-esteem, gluttony, envy, sexual fantasies or jealousy; you can become transformed if you're aware of it.

ONE FORM of journaling is poetry. Poet, Robert Bly, was quite fascinated with the shadow self. He wrote a poem where he explored an aspect of his thoughts regarding the shadow self.

I went off to see the moon on the piney hill.
Far in the woods, I sit against a pine.
The moon has her porches turned to face the light

but the deep part of her house is in the darkness.

YOU MUST'VE NOTICED his allusion to the shadow self and the persona. For example, the persona or our outward self which we love to show the world is described in the line "the moon has her porches to face the light". What do you think about this? Just like the moon, we often love to show the bright, comfortable parts of us; however, there's the darker part which we prefer to suppress. The moon, like us, knows that "the deep part of her house is in the darkness."

Two sets of activities along with prompts will be provided for you. The first will be carried out within a week, while the second set will be used to guide you in future shadow work exercises.

AHEAD, are the first set of activities to guide you in journaling your shadow. A total of 14 activities have been organized for you along with the perfect prompts to go with it. You can take two activities per day for the next 7 days. For each day, take one activity in the morning and the second in the evening.

LET'S GET DOWN TO WORK

Guided Activity 1. Day 1

BRING yourself into a calm state by centering yourself. Try to tap into your psyche. Become more aware. You can achieve this by doing any of these: doing breathing exercises, doing yoga, lighting a candle, meditating, having a cup of tea, jogging, or taking a walk.

Once you've done this, pick a pen and a notepad.

Poetry Activity

Write a poem to your shadow self. Assume it was a child lost in the woods. Connect your soul to your words as you beckon to him, or her. Engage all the knowledge you have about him, or her, so that as it listens to your voice, it recognizes it. Paint your pain with your words, bring your trauma to life with any words that flows from the stream of your heart.

Furthermore, as you write, wander around the events of today that remind you of your shadow. You don't have to be a skilled poet to make meaning out of the luxury of words in your possession. The meaning will surely be visible as you draw the poem to a conclusion.

Be spontaneous. Write as many words as you can.

Now that you've done this, let's try the next activity.

Guided Activity 2. Day 1

In this activity, you'll try to write about your experiences today. But this time, you'll write it in prose form. Below are journaling prompts to guide you as you write about today.

- Is there any action or behavior of someone that upset you today? Do you see this person's trait or behavior in yourself? How did you discover this person's behavior? Was there an argument, a fight, or an issue?
- Try to recall and then write about an experience that got you emotionally charged. Did it trigger your shadow self?
- Think of something you're in denial of

and then write about it. How long have you been in denial of this thing?

- Try to recall a time or situation where a friend, a colleague, a family member, or a stranger used a negative label on you. Maybe you were called stupid, over-sensitive, domineering, bossy, short-sighted, judgmental, or narcissistic. Did the things they said play a role in what you became? How?

You don't have to fret about the number of prompts. It can be overwhelming writing everything at a go; therefore, you can take them one at a time.

Before you get to the next activity, let's try to highlight and recall some of the possible shadow traits you might encounter. As we do this, try and see if any of them tallies with anything you observed about yourself today.

- Anger
- Outbursts of rage
- Envy
- Jealousy
- Manipulative tendencies
- Exploitative
- Arrogance

- Egotism
- Narcissism
- Obsession with yourself and your appearance
- Intolerant
- Judgmental
- Defensive
- Overly competitive
- Stubborn

Remember also, that the essence of this journaling experience is to help you dive deeply into your subconscious to understand your past and present better.

The journaling experience so far has helped you release some of the energy of your environment that you may have soaked up in the past or even the present.

Guided Activity 3 Day 2

- Try to recall one time you remember feeling wronged as a child. What was your reaction? Does this experience still affect you right now as an adult? What way does it affect you?

SUGGESTION: you may use simple paragraphs to write about each item. Remember, as you do this, try to connect with your emotions.

GUIDED Activity 4 Day 2

- Is there a time you felt betrayed? Write one or two things you'd like to say to the person who broke your trust. Be very honest about your feelings towards this person, as you write, imagine you'd see that person in the next few minutes.

GUIDED Activity 5 Day 3

- Think of one time someone you once looked up to let you down. Write about this experience and how you have felt since then. Write about the extent to which it affected you. Was the effect great? Was the effect mild?

GUIDED Activity 6 Day 3

- Write about a trait you see in other people that you wished you had. Also, write about why you think you don't possess this characteristic yourself.

GUIDED Activity 7 Day 4

- How often do you find yourself overthinking something you said in the past or something you've done? Can you also identify the triggers? Write about this.

GUIDED activity 8 Day 4

- Write down some of your core principles as a person or the things you value most. You may arrange them according to how important they are to you.

GUIDED **Activity 9 Day 5**

- Can you identify what could likely trigger envy in you? Write it down in the form of a list. Also, write down why you think this happens.

GUIDED **Activity 10 Day 5**

- What are the things you notice about you that make you realize that your mental health is dipping? Write them down. Try not to leave out any detail here.

GUIDED **Activity 11 Day 6**

- Write down the times you remember being hard on yourself? Why were you hard on yourself on these occasions? Where do you think this originates from? Why are you often under some pressure?

Do you feel you can be kinder to yourself? How do you think you can be kinder to yourself?

Guided Activity 12 Day 6

- Write about your reactions whenever you get angry. As you write, try to also indicate if your reactions when provoked are similar to the way other people who have been in your life react, whenever they're angry. Is there a reason for the similarity or differences?

Guided Activity 13 Day 7

- Write down what you think about failure. What are your perceptions about it? How do you define failure? How do you feel when you experience failure? Do you have any fear of failure? How did the people who raised you react to failure?

Guided Activity 14 Day 7

- Are there toxic traits you recognized in your parents or guardians? How do these traits manifest? How did you feel the moment you realized that your parents weren't perfect? Do you possess your parents' or guardians' toxic traits? What are your toxic traits if they're different, and how do you project these traits to others?

What More and What Not?

REMEMBER that shadow work is a form of self-care. May I remind you again that your effort to journal your shadow will help you restore and integrate your shadow selves that may have been repressed in the past?

As you begin to discover these elements of yourself, do not judge yourself or be too self-critical. If you are, you'll only send this part of your back to hiding. And this will be the wrong approach to take as it'll likely cause you to have mental issues such as anxiety and depression. The result again is that you may become inefficient and ineffective in your business, work, and family relationship.

Even as you have written these journals, always take your time to reflect on each item you have written and monitor your progress.

Remember also that you must hold yourself accountable for your actions as you're starting to take note of them. Call out your bullshit as soon as you find yourself engaging in toxic behaviors that affect yourself or other people. Hopefully that didn't offend you. But that is how to you have to be. Even as you call yourself out, try to understand, by exploring, why you acted the way you did. This is essential.

Do you know that your shadow will also show up in the form of self-sabotage?

REMEMBER to revisit these prompts as they're a good way to identify your weakness and help you achieve the growth you deserve.

JOURNALING ACTIVITIES: SECOND SET

These new sets of prompts for your journal can be used after the first week. They were suggested by renowned shadow expert and writer, Kate Tunstall. Some of them are slightly modified for you. Take your time to listen to them actively, and go through these one by one . Make sure to answer every question and do not skip any. It is okay if you have to come back to this section to write them down. At least listen to them and come back later to answer them. It will give you something to think about until then.

THINK about the people you're very close to. What would you like to change about them, if you had the power to, so that you can improve your relationship with them (this might also have to do with the way you resolve conflicts)? How does this action reflect on you? Based on this exercise, is there anything you could consider improving in yourself to help?

WHO HAVE you most let down in your lifetime, and how/why did it happen? Have you made peace with the situation? Write a letter to the person you disappointed telling them how you feel, even if you don't send it.

WHAT ONE THING could somebody say to you to bring you to your knees? Why do those words hold so much power? How can you begin to take the power out of those words?

WHAT COULD HAVE MADE your childhood better? How do you feel about that?

WHAT MAKES you self-conscious around others?

WHO HAVE you previously had a conflict with and allegedly resolved it, but you remain wary of since? How did they make you feel? What worries you about the relationship now?

WHO DO you hold a grudge against? What is stopping you from letting it go?

. . .

How do you feel about your childhood? Was it generally positive or negative? Who made you feel safe and who let you down? Who were you close to?

What is the worst emotion somebody could provoke in you? For example, anger, betrayal, jealousy. Why do you feel so strongly about this? Does your answer differ according to the person in question?

What's the worst character trait you have as a result of your childhood? What or who do you think caused it? How do you feel about that?

Which situation in your life do you most wish had a different outcome? How would it have improved your life? In what ways is your life better for it not to have worked out so?

What's your biggest regret in life? How might you be able to make peace with that? Think about your circumstances at the time and permit yourself to be okay with the fact that you did your best at the time.

WHO HAS LET you down the most in your life? Are they still around? How do you feel about that?

WHAT'S the worst thing you've ever done? What drove you to it? Have you confessed to your misdemeanor? Are you afraid of being honest? Examine why this is and whether if it's truly valid. Are you protecting yourself or others? Could being open about it help to bring you peace? How might you atone for it?

WELL, done! Feel any different?

ALL THROUGH THIS CHAPTER, our focus has been to help you journal your shadow self. While you've also learned how to use one of the most important aspects of shadow work, you've also learned to explore the dark side of yourself. There are many more exercises for you in this second part, but one lesson or motif for you in this chapter on journaling is this: don't throw away your journal. You'll need to look back at what's written and what progress you've made since your last journaling. Even if you've written based on some prompts, don't forget that they're still useful in the future.

MEDITATE. Meditation is a spiritual exercise. Nevertheless, the aspect of meditation here is where you spend a decent amount of time reading and thinking deeply about the issues you've written on for each prompt. That way, you're able to connect with these shadow selves and have a sort of psychic communion with them.

BELIEVE IN YOURSELF. Repeat. And then, embrace yourself.

Stay alert; there's even a lot more that awaits you in the next chapters as you continue your progress in your path to healing.

5
THE 4 STEP SOLUTION TO
HEALING YOUR PAST

*R*emember this: your goal is not to forget but to let go of the emotional connection of the memory forever.

In the previous chapters, you were guided through the mind of the shadow as well as how you can journal your shadow. You also must understand that you can only win when you know or understand your enemy. Well, since you now know who your shadow is, it'll be such an exciting adventure to find ways you can disconnect your emotions from your memory.

You'll learn, at this point, to let go of the emotional connection you have with the shadow consciousness, since you have learned to acknowledge its being. You know why? Because it is one of the steps to healing! Are you excited? Let's go!

. . .

QUICK QUESTION: How can I let go of the past and move forward with joy?

LET IT GO, but before you do that, learn the lessons and understand what the experiences cost you; remember and learn what it inflicted on you. Also, know this: letting go doesn't involve just dropping your baggage from the past.

There's an important question you'll need to ask yourself as you proceed: "How committed am I to healing?" Your response to this question will determine the extent to which you'll go to achieve healing.

How often have you heard people say, "You need to live in the present moment"? Perhaps even more often than I have. But it doesn't make this truth boring, nor does it make it irrelevant. The challenge is in answering the questions, "How do we accomplish this?" and "How do you live in the present and, why?"

You can begin to live in the present by making your life less complicated. In simpler terms, simplify your life. Joshua Becker is a coach, writer, and journalist who writes on becoming a minimalist. One of the things he recommends in living a simplistic life is that we eliminate unnecessary possessions. Does that mean that we throw away our physical possessions such as our cars, jewelry, or achievements?

Well, not really. The possessions he refers to are the inner baggage that slows us as we run the race of life. These loads still connect us to the emotions associated with our past lives and therefore need to be dropped. This is what helps you live a simple, easy life; this is what helps you enjoy the moment.

Therefore, how does the above relate to healing your past? Well, to heal your past, you will learn to live in the moment. And to do this means that you'd have to stop worrying about the past or the future. Consequently, you ought to enjoy the present and live for today.

Furthermore, as you choose to live in the past or the future, you deny yourself the enjoyment of the present. After all, the reason why many of us worry about the future and the past is that we want to achieve some enjoyment or pleasure or victory; whereas today's victory awaits us to celebrate, to embrace, and to revel in!

Now, let's find out how to heal your past in these 4 simple steps. But remember as you proceed: 90% of the work is done as you commit to healing.

#1: PRIME THE EGO

Think of the emotional pep talk a parent gives a child who is about to start a new school, or the pep talk a coach gives a substitute who is about to replace another team player during a soccer match where his team is trailing by 1 goal. The aim is to prepare them emotionally and mentally to be able to make a positive impact and deal with the pressure of adapting to a new situation and excelling in it.

Therefore, to prime your ego means to prepare it for the journey you're about to undertake. At this point, you must have known what your goal in this journey is, don't you? You'll need to reassure your ego about the work you're about to do. You need to convince your ego that the work you're going to do will contribute greatly to your healing. More so, you can engage in self-talk; you can engage in mantras or any form of meditation that will help prepare your ego for this journey.

THE OBJECTIVE IS to eliminate the doubts or uncertainties that can become a prevailing distraction to you. You could say to yourself, "Everything is OK, we need to heal, this is necessary, this must be done, this is for my highest benefit, and I'm going to live a joyful life after this, so it must be done." This is what you do when you prime your ego.

REMEMBER THIS: your ego is your self-protection mechanism. It's always protecting you or trying to protect you. The ego always tries to bypass emotional pain because it sees emotional pain the way your physical body sees fire. That is why it'll always want to bypass the healing process. Hence, prepping your ego as you face your thoughts is critical to healing. I'll help you remember this when we get to the fourth step.

#2: DWELL IN YOUR PRESENT STATE AND MOMENT.

Well, let me tell you this: you need to dwell in your emotion and cradle it; accept it and be present in your emotions and present moment. As you do this, smile. You need to acknowledge the fact that you're in full control of your attitude every day you wake up.

Therefore, you should be deliberate about this. Your smile will stem from how well you appreciate the moments of today. Revel in your victories from the day. Understand your mistakes and failures of today; face the battles of today.

What sort of moments can you have? You might be at work. It's a moment. Cherish it. Love it. You might be at school, learning a difficult course or subject, appreciate it and be positive about the outcome. Be present.

How can you be present even in the middle of all the distractions from the pain of the past or the uncertainty of the future?

Now, let's get to answering the question above for you. To be present even amid the distractions, here are 5 things you can do:

#1 BEING PRESENT. It's like an exercise. It doesn't fix you or give you the result you want immediately. **You must do it regularly to get that result**. So, the first step to achieving presence is to be present at first.

When you're present, you aren't worried about stuff like, "Oh, what did he think about my looks; do I look good enough?" or, "What did she mean when she made that remark?" All the distractions from what people think, how people speak or react, you are to let go.

THE RESULT WILL CERTAINLY BE that your social skills will improve as you deal with the anxiety that may have stopped you from being your true self. This is also important if you're struggling with confidence when communicating with people.

Assume rapport when you meet someone for the first time. This means that you assume that such a person is your best friend. This helps you eliminate the nervousness that may first come during the conversation. The foundation you set during conversations is key. And, this will also help improve your listening as you eliminate the noise from within. Be present. Repeat that and do it again.

#2 *DISCOURAGE yourself from thinking too far ahead.* Let's make this brief: when you think too far ahead, you become too conscious of yourself, and you may begin to second-guess yourself. Writer, Henrik Edberg, suggested that to improve your creativity, control your thoughts and prevent them from wandering too far ahead.

You may try to deliberately speak to yourself when

you feel your mind is wandering off. It is like you're giving yourself some instructions to follow.

APPRECIATE YOUR WORLD MORE. The more you antagonize your circumstances, the more you'll find it difficult to face. Therefore, take a deep breath. Stop labeling, analyzing, or judging the things and people around you. Appreciating the things and people around you are bold steps towards living more in the present. Look at the trees and the natural splendor they paint. Look at the positive colors of the people around you. Appreciate their smile, their gait, and even their humor.

TAKE *belly breaths and focus on them.* Doing this helps you release the stress that may come from being absent. Therefore, as you take a deep breath, count on each release. Focus on the breaths. Also, the counting you do on each release helps you achieve that focus.

TAKE ACTION TO GET STARTED. Every human is so unique. Find an action unique to you that can bring your wandering mind back to base, especially if you're a chronic overthinker. You may try to be present even for a while. This will truly relieve you of a moment's stress. Next, try to follow that up with more determined action-steps.

Do you know that there are many more benefits of dwelling in the present? Your ability to do this will open you up to a world filled with personal benefits. You'll worry less; you'll be more open; you'll be more playful; you'll be more cheerful, and the best of your colors will be released to paint the world like the rainbow paints the sky. Boy! That sure feels great!

#3 FACE YOUR Thoughts

Yes, bold pal, it's about time you faced your thoughts. Here's one for you: grieve. There's a lot you can do when you face your thoughts, but grieving is a by-product of that.

Well, here's something I did on one occasion. I was so buried in so much pain because there were things that had consistently not gone well for me. I was becoming depressed and hollow inside. It felt like I had a hole in my heart. I wanted to talk to someone, but I looked back at my history of sharing things with people and then I concluded that sharing might not be a good idea. As hard as I tried to force the pain and the hurtful thoughts off my chest, I just couldn't. It was at that moment I began a monologue with myself. I began to talk about how I felt for nearly 20 minutes. I began to expose the pain to space. I spoke outwardly, not inwardly, to the open space within my room. And as I spoke out my countless agonies and deeply buried pain, I started to experience some catharsis: all the emotional tensions I was feeling were being purged at that moment. They started to empty themselves. It's like that moment when you suddenly become bold enough to face a bully, then he or she realizes that you aren't as cowardly as he or she thought. The relief it brought me weeks later made me realize that fortune indeed favors the bold.

You could talk to someone about the pain you feel, but there's nothing wrong in talking to the outward space. Just assume someone was there listening. Nag into the ears of that invisible being. Yell! Mop! Say everything you think within. Good or bad, about yourself or not, just utter them with vehemence or calm, or whatever emotion that's inside you.

Now, after you've done this, distance yourself from your memories. If you have an emotional trigger to a thought or memory, distance yourself from it by breathing and allowing yourself to move forward and away from that thought. You could use a mantra. You could just say to yourself, "It's just a thought; it's just a memory." You can combine the mantra and breathing exercise.

Well, guess what you're doing when you try this? You're removing yourself from this emotional charge. Remember, memories are stored forever; however, the goal is not to forget these memories but to have no emotional pull from them.

Christina Lopes, an energy healer, spiritual teacher, and clinician said this:

> "you can't let go of your past without learning the lessons and understanding what the experience caused in them."

So, you see that your past is valuable to you; it isn't dead weight.

Think about what you've just read. Letting go is also a natural by-product of healing and you can't let go of something you haven't healed from.

Typically, when people let go, they don't heal first. People jump from the past to letting go, but this is wrong. We must heal first.

. . .

REMEMBER THIS: *letting go is a by-product of healing. You must heal first before you can truly be able to let go.*

TO TRULY LET GO, you have to go through the healing process. Stay with me here.

TRY TO ASK YOURSELF, "How do I heal the past?" It's the answers you find here that will lead to the outcome you seek. For instance, how do you truly forgive when you're still holding on to that painful experience? How do you let go of that painful experience when you haven't healed? Did you see the pattern here? Again, it'll be easier to forgive (let go) when you have learned to heal.

LET'S GET THIS STRAIGHT: *to heal from your past, you must learn to face your thoughts. To do that, remember what we said earlier in STEP ONE: your ego is your self-protection mechanism. It's always protecting you or trying to protect you. The ego always tries to bypass emotional pain because it sees emotional pain the way your physical body sees fire. That is why it'll always want to bypass the healing process. Therefore, prepping your ego as you face your thoughts is critical to healing.*

So, how can you heal? Take a meditative look at these two strategies:

FIRSTLY, engage your pain. Engage your anger. Engage your loneliness. Yes. Do so! I highlighted a personal experience with pain earlier on, and one thing I'm sure you took from there is this: by personalizing your pain, and by talking to your issue as though it were a person, you're easing yourself of the burden inside you. You're helping yourself heal. So, do remember to hold that soliloquy, that quiet, dramatic monologue where you vent to space as you're led.

SECONDLY, remember to embrace the pain. Have you ever tried to embrace someone you're mad at against your wish? I have. Funny, it had a magical effect on how I eventually felt towards that person. So, get to know your pain: embrace it. Love yourself through the process. Try to have an open heart. Try to grasp the memory: go head-on with it.

ACKNOWLEDGE the fact that you're the stronger person within yourself. Your shadow is merely the leftover of your light. You're the full light in your shadow. Believe in yourself: have faith. The battle will be won, and it includes the war with yourself. To truly grieve, you must accept death. Remember, nothing good comes easy.

#4: USE TONGLEN.

Tonglen is a Tibetan word meaning "giving and taking." It is also a type of ancient meditation or spiritual practice that helps you focus on compassion; that is, connecting with your compassionate self, developing it, and learning to apply it daily. It involves sending and receiving energy, taking in the negative (pain, suffering, fear, etc.), and giving back the positive (peace, joy, comfort, and well-being).

HERE ARE three simple steps to practice Tonglen:

STEP 1.

Get focused and dialed in (use the Indian meditation style only). Relax. Breathe. Sit down. Be comfortable. Quiet your mind. Ensure your palms are clasped together and drawn towards your chest and facing upwards towards your chin, but not close.

Step 2.

Focus your energy on the reality that someone is suffering the same pain as you. You could think of a friend, a spouse, a relative, or a neighbor. Imagine the difficulty they may be going through. Fix yourself in their anguish.

Step 3.

Breathe in their pain.

Remember: it is not only yours. You're not the only person suffering from this. The moment you recognize this, you'll expand with energy and vibrance.

Open your heart to compassion and empathy. Utilize breathing in and out of the pain. Breathe in pain and breathe out love, happiness, and peace to your heart and mind. Use your energy to reach others in the world who are experiencing the same pain. This will make you feel that someone is next to you – someone is by your side experiencing the same pain at the same moment which will comfort you in this challenging process.

Step 4.

Translate that darkness into light.

As you breathe out, imagine cleansing, purifying, and revitalizing that negative energy as well as turning it into the positive energy of love, self-healing, and acceptance.

Step 5.

Let the law of reciprocity play. Remember, you'll get back what you give to others. Remember the positive karma which states that "What goes around comes around 10-fold."

Imagine as you breathe out, that crystal white energy light is being sent to that person attached with peace, happiness, well-being, relaxation, protection, safety, freedom, and liberty.

You've done an amazing job so far; you've indeed come a long way. How did you find the exercises in this chapter? Can you evaluate your healing journey and measure your progress so far? Well, done. Now, get set for another journey as you get to learn how you can heal your inner childhood trauma.

6

HEALING YOUR INNER CHILDHOOD TRAUMA TECHNIQUE

As a person on a journey to healing, nothing you do will ever make as much sense as when you've come to understand your past experiences, control them, and wield them to your advantage. It is at this moment that you'll find peace with the questions that fester your mind about yourself – this has been one of our overriding themes so far here.

In this chapter, you'll learn to heal. You'll learn to believe again that healing is possible. We know this because the hope we allow ourselves to have before we start or continue a long adventure is what gives us that life, inner peace, and boldness to keep going. And, it's what I need you to feel at this moment as you continue the journey of healing.

First, let's talk about your inner child.

YOUR INNER CHILD

There's a child in every man and woman. No matter how serious, or pompous, or matured we are, there's a little boy or a little girl in each of us. Think of a time when you saw the rosy red cheek or dimple of a smiling child. Or when the warm, round and glowing sad eyes of a child looks at you. At that moment, your body begins to send messages to your brain, and you begin to connect the sorrowful look of that child to a memory of you as a child.

One thing you'll need to know is this: we all have an inner, lost child. It's the part of you that connects to pain when you see it in other people and then it reminds you of your traumas as a child. It reminds you of that part of You, which has been damaged, hurt, or locked in a closet for many years. It's this part of you that's often needy. It's this part of you that demands all the attention.

THE SHADOW SELF is sort of the reflection of this inner child. I describe this in the poem below:

In a fairly lit hallway,
A child sits alone
With a reflection of her that is visible,

But not her
Yet, this child,
She stretches her hand to the fissure
Where the light comes from.
She stretches her hand to the light;
She stretches her hands to you.

Your inner lost child is a reflection of you that was lost. It embodies your strengths and weaknesses as a child – the things you suppressed as a child because you were forced to. The times you were yelled at for behaving or acting in a certain way, but you decided you wanted to be free only to be lost again. The times you wanted to be loved properly, like every other child you knew, but you're forced to be content with what you got. It never mattered if you got little or nothing.

Of course, a lot of the pain, anger, rejection, and sadness would be retained by your inner child.

66 *"In every real man, a child is hidden that wants to play." - Friedrich Nietzsche*

The inner child and some components of it reside in your subconscious mind. However, the key to healing your inner child is to realize first that it has an energy house.

. . .

Now, let's dive into a little spirituality here.

The inner child lives energetically in the lower three chakras, but mainly in the first chakra. So, you'd need to understand what the first chakra is, and why the inner child lives there to heal it. I'll explain.

Now, the human body consists of 7 main chakras, but the main chakra we're interested in is the one located at the bottom: the first chakra. It is located at the base of your body, at the tip of your spine and down in the pubic area. This chakra is regarded as the root chakra because it is the foundation of your development. It's also the first chakra that develops in utero.

Your first chakra connects you to your first task after birth: "Do I belong to the world?" This fundamental question happens instinctively.

LET'S CONSIDER THIS. Psychologist, Erik Erickson, wrote on the stages of human development where he describes the several stages of it. In the first stage (trust versus mistrust), he makes a strong link with the base (first) chakra development.

· · ·

FOR INSTANCE, if you consistently experienced love and care from the people who raised you, then of course, you'd feel more secure in the world, and it'd be easier trusting people in the world. However, your perception about the world would be different if your caregivers were hostile, unloving, or if they provided you with little or no needs such as love, food, and emotional support. You'd end up lacking trust and faith in people as a result. You'd no longer be able to trust the world to be a place that can provide you with these good things. So, the truth is, the level of security, faith, or trust you have in mankind depends on your experiences as a child.

Also, the first chakra is the home of your inner child as I've stated earlier. It's a physical component that's about "a body". Its components are your 5 senses. Most children live in the consciousness of their 5 senses and that's why you'd notice that children are way more sensitive. They're connected to their 5 senses soon as they're born, and the 5 senses are connected to them. Therefore, your inner child lives in this body of emotions that serves as a warehouse for all the emotions you felt as a child growing up.

The inner child trauma you have can also be called your first chakra trauma. This is because they're both connected as stated earlier. And what this means is that, if you have inner child issues, then you've most certainly had first chakra issues, and if you've had first chakra issues, then you're having inner child issues.

Consequently, what goes on within the environment a child finds him or herself; will determine whether or not the child's chakra will end up impaired or to use another more descriptive word, dysfunctional.

Now, let's learn how you can heal your inner child's trauma.

TECHNIQUE #1: DISCOVER YOUR INNER CHILDHOOD TRAUMA

Now you know about your inner child, try to **connect with him or her**. It's easy. Just think of a memory. The earliest memory you can recall about yourself as a child would most likely be associated with a major event. It could be the time something amazing happened to you, or the time when something so traumatic happened to you.

Discovering your inner childhood trauma is the first step to healing. What are the things that consistently trigger thoughts of the past in you? If you observe closely, they're tied to one major setback you had as a child.

LET'S try these steps to help you discover more of your inner childhood trauma.

ON A NOTEPAD, write down as many things you hate about people. For example, "I hate people who're nosy."

WRITE down as many phobias you have.

WRITE down as many things or situations that may easily get you anxious.

WRITE down the few times you've felt there's something wrong with you.

WRITE down the times you felt unsafe as a child.

SIGNS YOU HAVE AN INNER CHILD TRAUMA

- You have phobias.
- You often feel abandoned or rejected by the people around you.
- You love attention, and you feel betrayed when you don't get it.
- You're a perfectionist, and you treat every mistake you make as failure or inadequacy on your part.
- You mistrust people.
- You find it hard opening up. You'd rather hide your feelings and emotions rather than talk about them.
- You hardly let go of toxic people or relationships. You'd rather hold on to them.
- You experience an identity crisis.
- You're usually a people pleaser as it gives you more comfort when people are on good terms with you. You can't risk losing a relationship.
- You easily get into fights with people.

There's a lot more to add to the list above, but it

helps to be reminded that a lot of the things we do come from the place of trauma.

TECHNIQUE #2: BECOME AWARE OF YOUR INNER CHILD

Another step to take to heal your inner childhood traumas is to be aware of your inner child. It's at this point that you become a parent to this child. You may listen to yourself talk about the things that held you back growing up. And then you listen to yourself pour out all the pains you can recollect from your childhood experiences. As you do this, imagine you're the parent listening and assume you're the child speaking.

You should have a dialogue with this child. Ask this child about the things that made her insecure as a child and listen as she narrates in her little innocent voice.

Your inner child needs, above everything else, "to be seen, loved and heard." So, you need to see them, love them, and care for them. It's a process psychologists refer to as re-parenting. This activity will help you achieve that.

. . .

ALSO TAKE NOTE OF THIS: the moment you become aware of a thing, it becomes present, or in other words, you come into the consciousness of it. Therefore, as you get to know your inner child through this heart-to-heart dialogue, she becomes conscious and present. This makes it easier to heal her trauma. Therefore, you're doing 70% of healing by following this first step. Now I am not being bias when I say the child is a her, it could be a him for the men or whomever you identify as.

TECHNIQUE #3: DO FIRST CHAKRA WORK.

Yes, it's also worthy of note that you can heal your inner child by combining both chakra work and psychotherapy. As I've mentioned earlier, there's a strong connection between the inner child and the first chakra; therefore, if the first chakra isn't worked on, your inner child won't be healed. It's not enough to just do psychotherapy: combine both.

How TO DO **First Chakra Work**

GROUNDING. To do this, take off your shoes. Stand on the bare earth and then begin to stomp your feet on the ground. As you continue to do this, you're helping to ground your first chakra. In addition, you could do grounding meditation. As you meditate, you could imagine roots coming out of the first chakra and then plunging deep into the earth as they ground the planet. This visualization meditation helps in grounding. Create a mental imagery of a root coming out, then going back into the earth, grounding the planet.

REASSESSMENT OF BELIEFS AND PROGRAMMING. You learned earlier on that the first chakra contains your early childhood experiences. You were taught to have certain beliefs about religion, race, culture, and even gender against your own will. The first chakra houses all data and programming for any group from generation to generation. All of these influence how each of these groups think, what they believe, and how they view life.

It's these beliefs that we're born into and forced to accept the moment we're born into this world that we eventually grow into. Hence, we need to reevaluate and decide whether or not they're healthy for us going forward. Because we didn't have the intellect and enough knowledge to decide which belief system was good for us; we accepted both the good and bad notions of gender, race, religion and culture.

Now that we are older, more intelligent, and even more aware, we can now reassess all of these notions and make more informed choices.

To be able to do this:

1. Write down all the core beliefs of your family.
2. Be open minded and objective about them. No matter how negative they are, they don't define you. The idea is for you to bring them to the fore and heal from them. This process will help you improve yourself and even your group.
3. Remember, you don't only have negative beliefs. There's also positive believes, but your focus is on getting rid of just the negative beliefs.
4. Meditate on these negative beliefs and ask your spirit guides to help you heal from them. All you need to do is just mention the negative codes you want to be removed from your first chakra and be conscious as you do this.

TECHNIQUE #4: ENGAGE IN MANTRA WORK.

The mantra work is a very powerful way to heal your inner childhood self. Remember that your inner child is supposed to be a source of positive energy; she's supposed to be a source of joy. When she becomes anxious, uncared for or abandoned, she can impair your life, hurt your relationships, or affect your attitude to your job or the things you love doing.

Imagine a child that's become unruly, unsettled and difficult to manage as a result. If, as a parent, you deal with that child aggressively, you'll only make the situation worse. You'll hurt your relationship with that child and that itself will steal your joy and fulfillment as a guardian. So, if we can't find strategies to get along with our inner child, we'll be unable to find the peace and fulfilment we seek.

Therefore, mantra work becomes a perfect strategy to calming the inner child, getting along with it, being in charge, and healing. You may develop simple mantras for yourself, but let me suggest a few for you below.

"WE'RE SAFE."

.   .   .

"Everything is OK."

"We're alright"

"You're loved."

"What do you need from me?"

"We're not in danger."

According to research, positive affirmations or mantras like the above will help you feel less anxious. Also, it helps you become more aware of your thought patterns and processes. When you say these mantras, remember to meditate on them. We can't say too much about the importance of meditation, but it is very important for every aspect of your healing process.

TECHNIQUE #5: GUIDED MEDITATIONS

Sometimes, your inner child can be severely wounded that it recedes to the depth of your subconscious. At this point, it might become difficult to access her. Doing guided meditation can help you in having access to her again. You can find some inner child guided meditations on YouTube. There are also mobile apps that can help you guide you through child meditation and healing.

You can just get your headphones on, find some inner child guided meditations, and be locked in. I'll suggest using noise cancellation headphones. Listen with your heart connected as the voice guides you through the meditation experience.

REMEMBER that our bodies hold amazing particles of good, compassion, and love, but all of these may be suppressed so that we may be unable to experience them. Guided meditation will help you reach even more to these.

Look at the ideas for meditation below and allow them to guide you as you meditate.

. . .

DRAW from your substance of love and support. Think of the people that spur love in your heart. Think of the place that spur love in your heart. Recall the beautiful memories of love, the things and the places that connect your heart to this beautiful feeling. As you do this, remember that even a little matchstick and paper can start a big fire. Let's assume that fire is your love. It is the little things you think about that start the great things you become. Become the love you wish you had by letting it fill your heart and consciousness.

GIVE YOUR BODY SOME ATTENTION. As you feel the positive sensations, as you draw from the positive substances, attend to your body. It is the first foundation to being mindful and conscious. Find a comfortable position. Relax. Don't be distracted, but become aware of your body and your breath. Grant your body a warm invitation. Invite it to rest. To feel relaxed and free. Then slowly relax into a sitting position. Zen master, poet, peace activist, and global spiritual leader, Thich Nhat Hanhn, says: "We stop, we calm, we rest, we heal, and we transform" because these help us to keep our appointment with life.

．　．　．

OFFER LOVE; offer compassion to your inner child.

USE the words below to silently invite your inner child and offer your love to her:

As I breathe in, I'm aware
As I breathe out, I'm aware still
I'm conscious of the breaths I take in
I'm conscious of the breaths I let out.
As I breathe in, I'm aware of my whole body
I become aware of my inner child-self
Hidden in the silent hallway of my subconscious
As I breathe in, I see myself in that subconscious
hollow-way
As I breathe out, I see myself stretching out to my 5-
year-old self
As I breathe in, I stretch my hands to her
As I breathe out, I stretch my arms to her,
This fragile, sad, lonely, abandoned child
As I breathe in, I embrace her
As I breathe out, I acknowledge she's me.

TECHNIQUE #6: DO INTEGRATION EXERCISES.

When we go through trauma in our childhood, we start to dissociate and disintegrate. The crucial part of healing is integrating these disintegrated parts. Bring all your broken parts back to wholeness then embrace and love them. Bring them into your consciousness. Integration exercises are very important to the healing process.

HERE'RE some exercises I've provided for you below to help you do the integration exercise:

PUT on some meditation music

WRITE down a prayer or a creed for yourself.

DECLARE THAT YOU'RE HEALING, and you'll be fully healed in your world.

. . .

SAY TO YOURSELF: "I'm committed to healing my inner child wounds," "I intend to bring my inner child along with her wounds into union," "I'm so loved," "I'm so honored," and "It is done!"

YOU'VE COME this far because you chose to. At this point, you'll need to commend yourself for the amount of effort you've put in to heal and be the best version of yourself. Well, done. Remember this, the journey to healing is a continuous exercise. We don't stop taking care of our health as soon as we complete a medication, instead we keep doing the things that'll keep us healthy such as eating the right food and doing the right exercises that will help us stay healthy. The same applies to shadow work. The process is continuous.

7

PEACE BE SHADOW THEREFORE
PEACE BE STILL

3 STEPS TO ACHIEVE THIS

*J*n this chapter, you'll learn the basic steps you can take to own your shadow. You've learned a lot about your shadow self in the previous chapters leading up to this, and so far, so good, I've been able to successfully help you harness your shadow energy by helping you come to terms with it. Knowledge is the first step to healing your pain. And, as I've stated at the beginning of the second part of this journey, my goal is to focus on the practical steps you can take to succeed in this journey to full healing.

Remember, your goal is to achieve peace with your shadow; your goal is to calm the unsettled sea raging inside of you. Are you ready? Because I am.

. . .

To GET a full understanding of the healing process you have to take basic steps that will guarantee your healing as long as they are followed. Now, you'll learn about some of the basic steps you can take to owning your shadow. These are practical steps that'll demand your actual compliance and commitment.

3-STEP GUIDE TO OWNING YOUR SHADOW AND ACHIEVING PEACE

Step I - Find your shadow

THE FIRST STEP to owning your shadow is to find your shadow. I can't overemphasize how important this is. As I've stated in previous chapters of this book, we all have a shadow, but we don't or may not be fully aware of all the materials or characteristics that constitute our shadow. We discussed some of the steps to finding your shadow in chapter 3.

#1. Monitor your most common criticism of others:

As you monitor or track the things you condemn in other people, you'll come to realize that those are the things you're dealing with personally but haven't been able to acknowledge. Recall what you read about projections? Yes, we tend to project our weaknesses on other people. Therefore, when you pay attention to the things you judge in other people (be very open minded, objective and honest as you do this), you'll see the elements of yourself that you didn't know you had before.

TO DO THIS PROPERLY, here are some strategies I'll suggest for you.

GET sticky notes of different colors.

ON EACH STICKY NOTE, write a person's name and one thing you've projected on him or her.

STICK each of the notes on a wall in your room. You can make sure only you have access to them.

EACH EVENING, as the day closes, add more to your list.

· · ·

EACH MORNING, spend a little time looking at your list, then at the end of each week, search, criticize and/or analyze yourself to see if you've at some point during the week shown any of these flaws or characteristics you condemned in these people. If you have, then write them down.

#2. Take mental notes of the people and things that frustrate you like hell:

YES, it's like carrying out a scientific experiment on yourself. Jotting down your observations will help you find the answers you seek about yourself. When you have taken these notes and observed them carefully, you'll realize that you find these things or people irritating because they embody characteristics you've repressed your entire life.

For instance, do people who show bigotry of any kind irritate you? Then ask yourself, "What ways can I exhibit bigotry? Or, have I shown bigotry in the past?"

.   .   .

DO AGGRESSIVE PEOPLE SCARE YOU? You might want to consider ways that you might have been violent towards people.

DOES someone yelling at you piss you off? Think of the times you might have reacted angrily to someone over something, or the times you voiced your anger loudly to someone for somewhat raising their voice at you.

#3. **Engage in freedom writing**:

IT'S true that there's always an element of oneself in his or her writing. Pick a poem and read. After reading this poem, read about the poet's biography or experiences. You'll find fragments or even more than just fragments of the poet in his work. Same applies to writers of other genres such as prose fiction or nonfiction.

Writing just about anything can lead us to the deepest parts of ourselves. Even the parts we surprisingly didn't know existed before, or the pasts we've forgotten. Your writing doesn't have to capture just one genre. You could observe the actions of people around you and write about it. You could also think about life and write about your perception of your reality or reality in general.

If you're struggling to come up with other creative writing ideas, you can find a song you know that can help you work. Music is food to creativity of which writing is part of. You can search for specific songs that can help arouse your creative spark.

Once you've found a song that brings your muse to life, think of the things that bother you the most about yourself. Fit it into a character for a short story of maybe 1,000 words or less. You could make it a character for a poem instead of a story supposing you find writing poetry easier. Be spontaneous while you write.

If you end up writing a story, observe your character and the things you wrote that he or she did. Of course, it might be fiction, but does he or she resemble you in any way? Are their actions familiar or relatable by coincidence or by intent?

#4. Do meditations and mantras; write prayers and creeds*:*

Meditations, for instance, are a crucial way to get into the deepest parts of your mind and so is mantra.

A lot has been written about these just to show you how important they are in finding your shadow and healing. Mantras are simply the words you say to aid your concentration as you meditate. Therefore, find positive mantras and say them as you meditate. In addition, use the guided inner child meditations you learned in the previous chapter to help you do this.

#5. Talk to and learn from someone experienced in the field of Shadow work, healing your life, or child trauma:

IT's important you learn from someone experienced in the field of shadow work. They will be able to guide you through experience and expertise. In addition, get into trauma therapy. Trauma therapy is the kind of therapy or treatment that can help you better handle the emotional response caused by a traumatic experience.

TRAUMA THERAPY CAN HELP you deal with experiences of abuse, abandonment, accidents, bullying, illnesses etc. To encourage you to try out trauma therapy, let me share with you some trauma therapy techniques that can help you find and manage trauma below:

IMAGINAL EXPOSURE IS an exposure technique where you're asked to imagine the trauma and tell it to your therapist.

IN VIVO EXPOSURE is another kind of exposure technique; however, it happens in real life, outside the therapy session. The goal of this technique is to help you approach the every-day activities you normally avoid because of their association to a certain trauma you faced.

WRITTEN account is where your therapist instructs you to write down your traumatic experience.

IMPACT STATEMENT IS a technique that involves you writing about why you think that experience happened and its impact on you.

. . .

COGNITIVE RESTRUCTURING STRATEGIES is a technique that will help you change helpful thoughts into more helpful thoughts

#6. Get into a group where people understand and are going through what you're going through:

THIS GROUP COULD BE about shadow work or the same traumatizing issues you're experiencing. Some groups may be focused on specific issues such as, sexual abuse, loss, death, pain, hurt, grief, terror, alcoholism, drug abuse, etc. This sort of group-based talk therapy helps a lot in unravelling the deepest part of yourself.

Another way group therapy helps is that, while you listen to other people share their trauma, you can begin to discover aspects of yourself through their words which you never knew existed. It'll also encourage you to open up about many of the things you've tried to hold back in the past.

#7. Get into an intimate relationship:

. . .

That is, get into an intimate relationship with yourself. To do this, you must pay attention to what lies inside your consciousness. Love seeks attention, and that attention must be given to your subconscious self. You can only get to find more about a person when you're attentive to them. What better way to find more about your hidden self than to be in an intimate relationship with him or her?

So, intimacy requires looking into the deepest part of someone, or something. It demands unravelling deep secrets; it requires exposing what we'd have otherwise hidden from others to this special person because of what you both share. It's this intimacy that you should have with yourself. You should be able to love yourself enough to be able to get to this stage.

STEP II - MAKE PEACE WITH YOUR SHADOW

When you've found your shadow, make peace with her. This is another step to owning your shadow.

IN THE PREVIOUS CHAPTER, we learned about the inner child, and why it's important to be in charge of him or her. You learned that if you aren't in control, she'll ruin your life because she'd then be the one in control. Also, we learned that the first step to being in control is to make peace with her. Now, here are several things you can do to help you make peace with some specific shadow personalities.

Aggression - Reconnect with Your Aggressive Instincts

In contemporary society, the word aggression typically means violence, warfare, and destruction. In other words, we focus mainly on one side of the aggressive coin. However, there's a healthy form of aggression important to both our psychological health and survival. It's this form of aggression that fuels your sense of self ownership. It encourages you in the face of fear. It's the motivation to explore and master the world outside of you.

Aggression is innate, and it comes from a human characteristic which is the tendency to grow and understand life better. So, how does anger, hate, rage, or even destruction become connected with it? Well, these negative aggressions become connected to it when this life force is obstructed in its development. Many people had their life force obstructed early in their development. Therefore, to adapt to this change, we had to repress this shadow side, and the result is that we've become susceptible to anger, hate and rage.

So, if we've repressed our aggressions into our shadow, can we assimilate it in a way that alleviates our anger and helps us improve our character? There's no general effective technique for assimilating or reconnecting your shadow.

However, to assimilate or connect with your anger, follow these steps:

TAKE SERIOUSLY the existence of the shadow.

BE aware of its qualities and intentions (pay attention to your moods, intentions, impulses and fantasies).

NEGOTIATE WITH YOUR SHADOW.

SEEK out safe and controlled productive outlets in which you can exercise your aggression. You can engage in a competitive sport, exercise or do martial arts. This will help you reconnect with your aggressive instincts.

WORK ON BECOMING MORE assertive in your behavior, more decisive in your choices, and more inclined to stand your ground when tested by people around you.

Doing this will help you channel your positive energy the right way. For example, rather than being forceful, you'll act with force; rather than being a dangerous criminal, you'll be potentially dangerous; and you'll be able to stand up for yourself and the things you believe in, instead of just being vicious and mean.

GREED - ACKNOWLEDGE the Greed in You.

Acknowledging the greed inside of you is one way to owning up to it. Of course, you don't have to become greedy as soon as the next tempting situation arises.

However, one thing you can do is to **think about the times you've been greedy.** Now, to explore this with you, let me simply describe a psychological process and exercise for you called, "Don't-think-of-a-pink-elephant".

For the next 45 seconds, try to think of anything that interests you. You can think about your day, the people you met today, your plans for tomorrow, or life generally. However, DON'T think about a pink elephant. Ready? okay go! You have 1 minute.

DID YOU SUCCEED? It's possible it didn't take you more than 5 seconds before the thought of a pink elephant came into your mind.

Well, this strategy is used by psychologists, and it's called an ironic process strategy. It was coined by a social psychologist and professor of psychology at the University of Harvard. He discovered that simply asking someone to avoid an intrusive thought fuels further obsession with that thought. People will try to repress these thoughts they've been asked not to think about and in the process create a conflict with that thought which means they'll have to think about that thought against their wish.

So, in order to avoid this conflict that you have with this dark part of you, you'll have to acknowledge its existence by making yourself think about it. The way to do this is to remind yourself of the times you showed elements of greed. Do this every day until you notice more consistent improvements.

If you reject the existence of this part of you, or try to even rationalize it, it'll only manifest itself in more damaging ways.

Say to yourself: "I know I'm greedy. Yes, I am greedy. I am greedy." Repeat this often until it no longer stings.

Once you've done that, say to yourself: "Although I know I'm greedy, I also know that I'm very kind and generous." As you consistently make yourself think about these aspects of you, you'll begin to integrate it and eventually find peace with yourself.

Bitterness, Envy and jealousy

These are shadows many people love to rationalize or reject. Who wants to admit they're envious of a person when they criticize how such a person spends money they earned or shows off his or her success? Who wants to admit they're bitter when they see someone from another race or gender do better than them and instead of acknowledging they're better or more qualified, they conclude that such a person achieved their success because of their gender, race, or ethnicity?

All of these aren't characteristics anyone can easily admit. The strategies you used to make peace with your greed can also be applied here. Personalize these characteristics and repeat them as you did above.

THERE ARE other strategies you can take to make peace with this part of you. Be prepared to write:

USING the journaling technique that you learned in chapter 4, write down any childhood memories you have about a time you became jealous of a sibling, classmate, or friend because they got more attention or favors from someone dear to you.

THINK of the times someone may have called you out for being jealous, envious, or bitter. Were their remarks justified? What did you do?

. . .

THINK of one time you were bitter, envious, and jealous without the object of your jealousy, envy or bitterness being aware.

THINK of one time you acknowledged, on your own, that you were envious, jealous or bitter.

THINK of the people in your life, friends or strangers that you may have observed or judged to be jealous or envious. As you recall their actions, do you still find them envious or bitter? Or just misunderstood?

WRITE a short poem focusing on how you feel about jealousy, envy and bitterness.

IF WE CAN EXTRAPOLATE the shadow owning methods just outlined, and use it to integrate other shadow characteristics, even those tied to your sexuality, creativity, narcissism, ambition or greed for power, you'll become more grounded and secure in your skin, and independent in your moral judgment. You'll also become more courageous and self-reliant; you'll

be able to achieve the ideal of psychological wholeness: the ideal that produces the greatness of character that many seek in this modern world today.

STEP III - JOURNALING YOUR SHADOW

One strategy to owning and taking charge of your
shadow and ultimately achieving the peace you
deserve is to journal your shadow. Journaling your
shadow will also help you achieve number one in
this guide, which is, *finding your shadow*.

A lot has been written about shadow journaling
in chapter 4 and how you can journal your shadow.
Think of the things you do to keep a new relationship going. Communication seems to be the most
important thing you do. You send texts. You call.
You send flowers. You send gifts. All of these are the
things people do to communicate with the people
they love.

So, journaling is a form of communicating with
your shadow self. This is how you exercise the
newfound intimacy you've created with your
shadow. As you write about your everyday shadow
experience, morning and evening, and as you write
about the things you struggle a lot to admit about
yourself, you're engaging your shadow; you're
bringing it to the fore; and you're taking charge.

What this means is, you're now going to take charge rather than let it take charge.

Journaling is a great way to spend more time with your shadow self. And, as you spend more time through journaling, you can learn more about him or her which will help you build your experience with your shadow. As you build your shadow experience, you become a master in handling him or her.

Don't just write; meditate on what you've written. Again, we talk about meditation. It's one of the most important aspects of shadow work, and everything you do in the shadow work experience will almost certainly come with meditation.

HERE ARE some things to know about journaling your shadow that'll encourage you:

- Journaling is a great way to exercise your shadow traits.
- Journaling helps to bring up the creative part of you.
- As you journal your shadow, you'll be taking a bold step towards acknowledging it. And acknowledging your shadow is a prime step towards healing.
- Your shadow is like your pen-pal. As you

write to it, you're keeping the relationship going, making it easier for you to bring it to a calm, less aggressive state.

- Journaling helps you bring your shadow self to your consciousness.
- Journaling will help you gain a lot more control over your shadow.

Throughout this chapter, you've been able to learn several steps you can take to finally owning your shadow and achieving peace and stillness. You can keep practicing and using these methods consistently. You can also find other strategies that work best for you. During the course of your week, you may also set aside a timetable of activities you can do, (and when you can do them), based on the items in this chapter.

As you do this, remind yourself that the best version of yourself will come.

8

ADVANCED PRACTICES FOR A SHADOW WORKER

Do you know that to improve your mind and to tap into the depths of your whole being, you'll need to gain some advanced spiritual knowledge? This is because your spirit is part of what forms your being, and nourishing it is one of the crucial steps to achieving wholeness and peace. There are a whole lot of spiritual practices that can help you in your shadow work journey.

In this chapter, my goal will be to help you dive into some of these mostly unheard-of spiritual practices which you can use to engage your shadow. Take note, these are advanced practices, but I'll try to simplify it as much as I can. What is most important is following the steps with courage and commitment.

Generally, shadow work is a spiritual exercise.

Much of what you've learned so far about connecting with your shadow self and reaching out to the darker part of you are real spiritual exercises necessary to engage the darker part of you. That is the part of your hidden subconscious. To engage this spiritual part of you, you must engage in spiritual practices. Your spirit is the non-physical part of you where your emotions and character sit. And, guess who is at the center of this? Yes, your guess is as good as mine.

Now, what are some of the advanced spiritual practices you can engage in to help you advance your healing? I'll help you here, don't worry. These practices are practical, and you should certainly try them while you read.

TONGLEN

I thought it'd be cool for us to start with tonglen spiritual practice although it's already been mentioned earlier in this book. This time around, you'll learn more about practicing tonglen. As earlier mentioned, it's an ancient practice that stemmed from Buddhist traditions. It's used in different contexts ranging from spiritual, to therapeutic, and then to secular. It's one spiritual exercise that sort of focuses on helping others as a pathway to also helping yourself. The Tibetan word, translated to English, literally means "sending and taking." Therefore, it's a spiritual practice that believes that the best form of gaining the peace you seek is giving it. And to achieve peace or to alleviate suffering, one must acknowledge the existence of it in oneself and others.

THE MAIN AIM of tonglen is to bring to life the compassion inside of each of us. We all have an element of compassion inside of us, and this includes the cruelest of us.

Your tonglen journey starts as you take on the suffering of others. Perhaps someone close to you or not, but whom you know to be suffering and needs help. It could be a young child in a hospital suffering from cancer. It could be a friend going through pain and trauma. It could be a family struggling.

We think of these people and breathe in their pain, and as we breathe out, we send out relief to their pain, healing to their wounds, and peace to their storm. As you breathe out, you send happiness and peace to that friend hurting. So, this is the core of tonglen practice that as you breathe in someone's pain, you breathe out relief to their burden, hope to their fears, and calm to their storm.

I understand that when you try to attempt this, you'll face obstacles. It's like holding a big bag over your neck and trying to help a struggling child relieve his baggage. You can be restrained a little by your fears, anger, pain, and struggles. But there's a way out of this.

AS YOUR THOUGHTS begin to drift towards your pain, focus on it. But this time, try to think of other people going through a similar burden like yours. Imagine they didn't have your kind of strength. Imagine some are already giving up. Imagine your pain in them and think of how they're handling their burden. At this point, you're doing tonglen for the other millions of people going through similar pain as yours. Whatever name you call your pain; you may call it anger. You may call it jealousy. You may call it revulsion.

Whatever you've accepted your pain to be; whatever you recognize it to be, others are feeling the same way as yourself, and so you channel your thoughts to them. You breathe in their pain again. You may not even know what you're feeling, but you do know that no man has a pain unique to only himself. We may respond differently, but we still have people who face the same things we face. So, you breathe in their pain. You take in the suffering both for yourself and for them and then breathe out hope and relief of the pain and suffering both for yourself and for them. You're the hero in this. They say not all heroes wear capes.

Usually, we seek after things on our terms even when getting them would hurt others. Sometimes, we want things to go out well for us without caring much about how things are for the guy next door. Tonglen brings down the walls of selfishness we've worked so hard to create. It demolishes the bulwarks we've spent our time and energy building. And, in the Buddhist tongue, we could call this dissolving the fixation and cling of ego. We become more collective than individualistic.

With tonglen, you don't avoid suffering nor do you seek pleasure: it's the reverse of it. Instead, you face suffering because the only way to overcome an obstacle is to face it. As you practice tonglen, you erase the long-standing tradition of selfishness; you become more aware that man thrives more as a collective than a selfish, individual being. You begin to feel a budding love for yourself, and it's from this love growing inside of you that you eventually spread to others.

. . .

TONGLEN AWAKENS A LOT of positive things inside of you such as your compassion and selflessness. You begin to understand life better. Your view of reality changes. You see how limitless the unlimited emptiness is, you see the unlimited void, and you see the limitless Sunyata space. It allows us to connect with a better aspect of our existence; we connect to a higher aspect of our being – a better one. This lets you learn that things are not as difficult as they appeared before.

You can do tonglen for the sick, the bereaved, those dying, people in anguish, or people in any form of distress. The unique thing about this exercise is that there's no restriction to where you can do it. If you find someone suffering, even in a subway, you could take a break to do tonglen for them. You can breathe in their pain and breathe out healing. As we see people go through pain, rather than feel helpless ourselves, we can use our challenges, suffering, and pain as a launch pad to help others through theirs.

I've described the tonglen practice for you to spur your spirit and to prepare it. Are you ready to practice it now?

.   .   .

THERE ARE four stages of tonglen practice. I'll guide you through the stages again. These stages are the formal stages of tonglen. Those described for you above are what you do in unexpected situations. Let's get started.

FIRST STEP.

TAKE a few seconds and become still. Allow your mind to rest. Think of a river. Then allow your mind to wander in the emptiness. Settle into the "voidness". Traditionally, we call this, "flashing on absolute bodhicitta". That is a spontaneous state where you wish for enlightenment and compassion for all sentient beings – all beings that have feelings and that are conscious. At this point, you're striving towards awakening, compassion, and empathy. You're opening to clarity.

SECOND STEP.

YOU ARE GOING to try to work with texture. At this point, you'll breathe in the light hot air. Breathe in the dark. Breathe in the feeling of claustrophobia. Once you've done this, breathe out warmth. Breathe out the cool, fresh, and relaxing breath of hope. Let the whole of your body, including your pores, release every breath you've taken in, but this time with positive, satisfying, and relieving breath. Continue this until you've completely synchronized both the ins and the outs of your breath.

Third step.

Recollect your painful personal circumstances and work with them. It's common that during the practice of Tonglen, you begin with working on someone else's painful situation. However, if you feel stifled, you can begin with working on yours then sliding into the pain of others in a similar circumstance as you. You should do this simultaneously. For instance, if you're feeling hopeless or scared, breathe in this sensation along with others who're feeling the same at that moment, then breathe out hope, comfort, and courage.

Lastly,

. . .

EXTEND what you've been taking in and sending out to a wider group. Suppose you've been doing Tonglen for someone dear to you, this time around, send it out to others suffering the same as the person dear to you (friend, partner, relative, or sibling). If you're doing tonglen for a person you see suffering on the streets, on TV, or for someone spoken of by a friend, then extend it from him or her to others in the same boat. You should make it go beyond just that one person.

You could do tonglen for those you may consider as your enemies, or for those who consider you, their enemy. Perhaps they may have hurt you or someone else in the past, but you still do tonglen for them. Because you know that the world will heal faster when we heal someone. We breathe in their pain and then breathe out healing because think of them as being in just as much pain as your dear ones and yourself.

There's no limit to who you can do tonglen for. It grows to an unlimited number. As you do tonglen, you become more compassionate with yourself, others and the world around you. You'll also begin to realize that the things you thought were rigid, aren't the way they appeared. The things you thought were solid, aren't. Even the unchanging things begin to transform. For example, the resentment, anger, or unease you used to feel towards others will now transform into love and compassion. And the ease with which you'll begin to give out these positive emotions will surprise even you. You'll learn ultimately that your tonglen exercise was able to awaken the positive emotions you didn't know were lying within you and even others.

SHAMATHA MEDITATION

Now, let's get to learn more about another shadow work practice which brings us to an exercise that evolved from Buddhist traditions, shamatha meditation. Although the word itself means peaceful abiding or tranquility, it's also called mindfulness or concentration. It's the first stage of practice that ultimately leads to the vipassana (insight meditation) practice. I'll guide you through the shamatha version practiced in the Vajrayana traditions.

So, what's the purpose of the shamatha practice? Well, people who engage in shamatha meditation want to stabilize their minds. And they do this by developing a consistent awareness of the focus of meditation. Traditionally, shamatha practice begins by using different kinds of support to carry out this practice. This eventually leads to meditating in an open area, with the emptiness visible, and without any form of support.

I'll guide you through how you can do shamatha meditation with your breaths as the focus.

SHAMATHA MEDITATIONS WILL GUIDE you through the depths of your mind. Then you'll be able to see your mind in its true nature. You'll see the kind of thoughts you have buried inside of you: both the good thoughts and the bad ones. You'll realize that you have a lot of thoughts inside of you that you didn't even know were there. However, remember that it isn't unnatural for you to have thought. As life goes, and as you experience life, all of these thoughts are born.

ONE BENEFIT of doing the shamatha meditation consistently is that you'll begin to experience peace in your mind and calm to your emotions. You'll experience pleasurable serenity inside your mind which will ultimately lead to your negative thoughts reducing.

As I mentioned earlier, the next stage of shamatha is vipassana, and you'll be ready for this stage once you've attained steady awareness. The vipassana will help you build your understanding of your mind. You'll be able to do this by learning the characteristics of your thoughts. The Vajrayana tradition's main goal is that you practice calm abiding and insight in union because this will open the door to learning the essence of your mind.

THE TRADITIONAL METHOD of teaching shamatha is we begin with some instructions on your physical body followed by you looking at the instructions of the meditation on your body. Now let's practice.

FIRST, let's begin with the seven-point posture of Vairochana.

TAKE A CROSS-LEGGED SITTING POSTURE.

GENTLY PLACE your hands on your knees or your lap.

ENSURE YOUR BACK IS STRAIGHTENED.

. . .

WIDEN YOUR SHOULDERS so that your heart center can be opened.

NOW LOWER YOUR JAW.

GENTLY OPEN your mouth and rest your tongue on the roof of the mouth.

KEEP your eyes open while you gaze at the widths of four fingers and then the tip of your nose.

AGAIN THE MAIN purpose of the multiple points posture is to cultivate a calm, attentive mind to enhance your meditation practice. Keep practicing until you get this right. It's okay if you don't at first.

NOW, let's look at another posture method focused on body sensitivity. So, we all have different bodies, it's good to adopt a body posture that meets the needs of our bodies so be sure to choose a traditional posture that is good for you. I am only giving you pointers and new insight. However, the most important thing to note is that you must in doing a body posture, ensure that your back and spine are straight and comfortable.

So, for a more sensitive body posture, these are the seven-point postures you can take:

First, you can lie down, or you can sit on a chair or cushion.

Your hands should be arranged in a comfortably stable way.

Your back should be held straight.

Relax your shoulders and open your chest.

Ensure your head is held at a comfortable level.

Open your lower jaw slightly.

. . .

YOU CAN CLOSE your eyes or open them.

NEXT, let's get to the meditation itself. We'll be focusing on the basic breath meditation from the Vajrayana tradition.

POSITION yourself in a way that you feel comfortable. Follow this up to be aware of your breath as you begin the practice. Focus on the breaths you take in and the breaths you exhale. Be conscious of your breaths.

WHILE YOU'RE conscious of your inhales and exhales, begin to release your thoughts as they arise. If you feel distracted at any moment by holding onto a thought, just refocus on your breaths. Repeat this as often as you can.

YOU'LL NOTICE your breath being released into space as you exhale. Try to experience the same thing as you inhale.

. . .

FOLLOW this up by letting your consciousness merge into the open spaciousness along with the breaths on each exhale and inhale.

NOW, try to intensify this practice by holding your breath for some seconds after breathing in. As you do this, you're dividing your breaths into three parts: the inhales, the held breaths, and the exhales. Continue to do this.

AT THIS POINT, you should chant to yourself with each inhale. Chant "ah" as you hold your breaths, and as you release your breath, chant "hung". It is believed that as you chant these sacred syllables, you become more aware, and your mind is purified in the process.

WHILE YOU EXHALE, try to relax more. Keep practicing on awareness, let go of your thoughts, and then return to your breaths. Carry on with this for as long as possible.

VIPASSANA

Let's get to another form of meditation that you can practice to help you in your shadow work journey. Again, choose the meditation that works for you. Not every meditation is for everyone, but everyone can do them if practiced.

This exercise is also spelled as vipashyana. As stated earlier, it's also known as "insight meditation". It's a traditional Buddhist meditation used to improve mindfulness. When you do this meditation, you'll focus on your innermost self in a way that's not judgemental.

VIPASSANA IS VERY beneficial for your mind and your body. The ancient Buddhist language of Pali translates Vipassana as "seeing things as they truly are." Literally, it means special seeing. Specifically, Vipassana involves observing your thoughts and emotions as they are. And as you do this, you do not dwell on them or judge them.

Other meditations like pranayama (where you practice regulating your breaths) or visualization (focusing on something specific such as an event, a person, an image, etc.) differ from it. In Vipassana, your focus is on your inner self. You don't attempt to take control of the experience. Let's now look at some of the goals of this practice. This method will:

- help your mind become quiet, still & relaxed.
- assist you to stop worrying about the future.
- help you stop being too bothered about the past and to stop regretting.
- aid in giving you a more realistic response to challenges and situations.
- help you focus more on the present.
- allow you to accept your thoughts, your feelings, or emotions as they are.

So, before you get to see how you can practice Vipassana, let's see some of the benefits of this exercise. First, Vipassana can help reduce stress. This is proven by a study conducted in 2014. At the end of the 6-months study conducted, among the participants, it was found that it was reduced compared to those who didn't participate in the exercise. The report also showed that Vipassana participants also experienced increased mindfulness, became self-kind, and improved their wellbeing. So, what are the general benefits? Let's see.

- The exercise improves mental wellness which can be shown in more self-acceptance, competence, engagement and growth, and positive relationships.
- When you practice Vipassana meditation, it can help you increase your brain plasticity.
- Research also shows that it can help treat addiction.

Let's see what it takes to practice this. Let's start with the beginners' steps.

IF YOU WANT A STEP-BY-STEP GUIDE, go to look up Vipassana meditation video recordings on YouTube. They're free. Or check out our website at www.goodselfhealinghabits.com

ALTERNATIVELY, you can find apps such as the balance on PlayStore, which contains recordings of guided meditations along with daily plans. Or, you can download the Dhamma.org app, which is a Vipassana meditation app. There, you'll find audio recordings, articles that are educational, and resources for Vipassana courses.

. . .

PARTICIPATE in a Vipassana meditation program for guidance that'll be tailored to your needs. You can find some personalized Vipassana classes in Yoga studios or spiritual classes.

REMEMBER to have a timer set at the beginning. When you've become more comfortable with the exercise, increase the timer.

SWITCH off your phone to reduce distractions. Ensure that those around you are aware that you'll be meditating to avoid being disturbed or interrupted.

YOU'LL HAVE to learn to be patient as patience is key to successful meditation. If you're new, remember that it will take some time before you become comfortable and used to the practice.

IF YOU DECIDE to try it at home alone, then I will assist in guiding you the best I can from here, with these 7 steps I have outlined for you.

STEP 1. Set time aside.

Recommended time: as soon as you wake up in the morning.

Duration: 10-15 minutes.

STEP 2. Find a quiet, serene area where you won't be distracted.

Where: A room where you'll be alone. A location outside where you can be alone.

STEP 3. Sit.

How: Have your legs crossed in a position you find comfortable. Be relaxed. Make your back straight.

STEP 4 CLOSE YOUR EYES. Breathe.

How: As you close your eyes, breathe normally and focus on your breath and the sensations you feel.

. . .

STEP 5. Pay attention to the exhales and inhales.

How: focus on your thoughts as you breathe in and out. Pay attention to your feelings and do not react or become critical of them.

STEP 6. Observe the distractions when they come. But return to your breath.

STEP 7. You can begin with 10-15 minutes of the exercise, but as you become comfortable, try to do up to 20 minutes or more of the exercise.

The bottom line is that all of these ancient exercises are very necessary for the shadow work journey. To become whole and achieve the best version of yourself, you should engage consistently in these spiritual exercises.

As we come to an end here, I want to remind you about the importance of journaling your thoughts. Too much can't be said about journaling, but one crucial thing to note here is that you'll become more in control of your shadow if you engage in more journaling. The next chapter is so important as it'll give you more insight on how journaling can reveal more about your shadow self.

9

131 PROMISING QUESTIONS TO ENTER FROM CONSCIOUSNESS TO SUBCONSCIOUSNESS AS YOU PLEASE

ell, done, you've started the last lap of this journey. Much of the thesis of this book has been that you can connect with your dark side and that connecting to your shadow self is a major step to healing. You now know that repressing these feelings will only lead to more problems in your relationships.

Furthermore, accessing your subconscious self and being acquainted with the lost child inside of you requires certain shadow exercises which we've focused on learning in part 2 of this book. For instance, in the previous chapter, you learned some practical ways to connect to your shadow self through some spiritual exercises. You also learned in previous chapters the role of journaling in accessing and creating a good relationship with your dark side.

Get set, because, in the chapter, we'll go ballistic in the shadow work exercise. We'll be focusing on very practical journaling exercises for you to get fully in touch with your shadow self.

WE'LL GUIDE you through this part with deep questions that you'll try to make journaling notes from. Your heart must be open, and you must be boldly honest with yourself as you go through each question. As many questions were provided for you to help you consistently practice conversing with your subconscious. If you took 1 question per day, you have enough to guide you through your journaling journey for the next 131 days. That is way more than enough time to build a healthy great habit for self-healing! I strongly encourage you to take your time on these and spread the questions out evenly so you don't overwhelm yourself! Practice safe Self-Healing Practices first and always :)

REMEMBER, our goal in shadow work is to reveal these shadows and learn to love and accept them. Ultimately, we'll let them go once we've achieved this so we can attain our greatest possible potential. Here are some questions to guide you through this process. Try to find a calm, quiet, and relaxed position, and connect your heart and your mind as you begin to go through the questions. The questions will be personalized at the beginning to help you connect better to their depths, but as you read them, speak to yourself.

Also when you are listening to these on audio, I want you to close your eyes and listen. Envision the question as you ask it, or as it is being asked, and allow the answers to come to you naturally using the breathing techniques mentions in all the chapters. There will be a very long pause for you to think about the question and answer accurately. When writing in your journal, make sure to rewrite the question so that you can feel the pain of the shadow release through your soul, through your hand, into the pen and onto the paper.

ARE YOU READY?

WRITING IN THE SHADOWS

When I think about power – all forms of it – what comes to mind?

. . .

WHAT SORT of connection do I have with power?

HOW EAGER AM I to gain power at the expense of others?

TO WHAT EXTENT do I seek power of any form?

DO I feel like I need to gain control over a sexual partner?

HOW DO I feel when I'm unable to gain control over a sexual partner?

DO I feel a strong desire to be controlled sexually by an intimate partner?

DO I feel superior to the people around me?

. . .

Do I feel like I'm incapable of being loved by someone?

Am I obsessed with wealth or money?

Do I feel like I'm damaged and irreparable?

Do I feel too broken to be fixed? Why do I feel this way?

What event could have created this feeling? How long have I felt this way?

Why do I aspire to be financially wealthy?

What's my attitude towards money and wealth?

When was the last time I used someone?

. . .

Do I feel like using someone? Can I think of the first time or the last time I had that feeling?

Do I OBJECTIFY SEXUALLY?

AM I MANIPULATIVE? Do I show the tendency to be manipulative? Do I gain pleasure in being manipulative?

WHAT ARE the things about women that I find repulsive?

AM I the sort of person that judges people at any slight opportunity?

AM I HATEFUL OF PEOPLE? What expressions or thoughts of mine which I've shared in the past appeared as hate to someone?

HAVE I wished death to anyone close to me?

. . .

HAVE I wished death to a popular person? Perhaps a celebrity, or a sports person?

WHAT CHARACTER TRAITS do I mostly find repulsive? Do I see them in the people around me? Have I shown these traits subtly or deliberately?

HOW DO PEOPLE SEE ME?

WHAT ARE my opinions about how people see me?

HOW WOULD my close friends and relatives describe me? Is it any different from the way a colleague at work, a classmate, or an acquaintance would describe me?

WHAT ARE THE THINGS, circumstances, or situations that can trigger me?

WHAT COULD TRIGGER the happiest thoughts and emotions in me?

. . .

IF I FACED the girl or boy 15 or 30 years ago, what would I say to him or her?

HOW I SPEND the rest of my life will depend highly on how I spend my life every day. What do I think about this?

HOW DOES a great day begin for me?

WHAT ARE the healthy ways I can manage my emotions?

HOW OFTEN DO I project myself to others?

WHAT'S my reaction like when things don't go as I plan?

DO I feel too honest with people about my feelings?

. . .

Do I feel ashamed after I've shared something about myself with someone else?

Where do my irrational thoughts come from?

What circumstances or situations can cause me to become judgmental?

Is there a certain behavioral pattern I notice on people that could cause me to become critical of them or to judge them?

How often do I feel let down? When last did I feel someone disappointed me or didn't live to my expectations?

Think of how I've reacted to being let down in the past. Did I find my reactions necessary? Were they rational?

Do I influence others easily?

Am I easily become influenced by people?

Is there anyone that has a very strong influence on my life, the way I think, and my decisions?

How often do I feel jealousy or envy?

Why do I feel envious?

Do I currently feel bitter about someone's success or achievement perhaps because they're showing off or it's getting them more attention than me?

What are the things I'm capable of doing to gain the things the people I am jealous of have?

EXCELLENT WORK SO FAR, THIS IS
GETTING DEEP. NOW LET'S GET EVEN
DEEPER.

Try to recall a relationship you ended or had to end. Has it been a great life choice for you? Try to write down some of the reasons why you feel it's a great life choice.

WHO HAS CAUSED the most pain in your life? What exactly did they do? Are they aware? Write them a letter, and in the letter, highlight the things you'd love to say to them.

WHAT COULD EASILY SCARE YOU? Are you willing to face your fears if they presented themselves right now? Do you know a safe way to approach your fears?

ARE there misconceptions people have about you? Are you certain of these misconceptions? Do you think you may have played a role in them having these misconceptions? How do you feel about people having misconceptions about you?

. . .

ARE there memories from the past that make you feel ashamed? Recall what you were like then, who you are, or the things you did. Have you changed much? Reflect on the extent of change you've attained since then. After you've done this, write these words – "I forgive myself because I've done the best that I could ever do."

CLOSE YOUR EYES and try to reflect again on the memories that cause you to feel shame. Try to picture yourself at that moment when you were on the brink of your existence. Picture yourself at that moment when you feel worthless, useless, or condemned. Find yourself again at that moment when you felt there was no way back for you because of the things you did. Now try to purge yourself of that feeling. Allow the catharsis to happen. Allow yourself to feel the emotions you first felt. After you've done this, consider how far you've come. Consider the progress you've made, and no matter how great or little the progress is, be happy about it and encourage yourself consistently.

. . .

THINK OF YOURSELF AS A SIBLING, a loved one, or an intimate friend. Release the compassion you'd have released to them to yourself if you found them in the same position as you. How would you have encouraged them? Do the same for yourself.

TAKE a pen and a paper and write a letter to your past self. In your letter, show kindness, understanding, and forgiveness. Be positive and encouraging.

ARE there traits you'd hate to be described as possessing? If so, why?

WHY DO you find these traits terrible?

HAVE your emotions ever been trivialized by anyone? When did this happen?

WHAT EMOTIONS CAN BRING out the worst character or response from you? Do you think there's a certain reason why this is the case?

. . .

HAVE YOU EVER BEEN SELF-DESTRUCTIVE, perhaps verbally or physically?

TRY to recollect how you felt at that time and the things that triggered this feeling.

HOW CAN you measure your relationship with people?

DO you have friends that you feel secure with? Are there others you feel less secure with?

DO you feel loved amongst your friends?

ARE there times you felt isolated?

DO YOU OFTEN FEEL ABANDONED?

DO you feel pressured or uncomfortable?

. . .

CAN you try to examine why you have this feeling? Does a past event play a significant role in why you feel this way?

THINK ABOUT YOUR RELATIONSHIPS. Which of them do you think is a disadvantage to you at this very moment? Write to the people you're in this sort of relationship with. Remember, you don't have to hide anything: your writing can only be seen by you, so be ruthless.

ARE you in a relationship that feels like an obligation to you?

HOW'D you feel if you ended the relationships that seem to drain you, or the ones you feel aren't beneficial to you?

DO you think those relationships are worthy of being salvaged assuming they're salvageable?

HOW CAN YOU SALVAGE THEM?

. . .

WHAT CAN you do to dissolve these relationships? What are the effects of dissolving them? Try to write a letter to that person you're in this relationship with and express how you feel about the relationship.

WHAT DO you dislike most about yourself? Why do you feel such dislike?

TRY to examine yourself and then see if you'd feel the same level of dislike, or even any dislike at all if you see someone show the same traits you dislike about yourself.

DO YOU FEEL MISUNDERSTOOD? What are the things you would like people to understand about you?

ARE there qualities about you that people ignore? How can you better demonstrate these qualities so they're more visible for them to see?

. . .

Do you have recurring nightmares? Can you describe what they're about? Are they linked to any event in your life, past or present?

In what ways can you face the cause or subject of your nightmares?

What's the most despicable thing you've done? Have you ever confessed to the terrible things you did before that no one knew you ever did?

Are you scared of honesty? Do you fear huge repercussions if you tell the truth about your misdemeanors? Or do you worry about your reputation if you told the truth about your misdemeanors? Why is this the case? Is this feeling justified? Do you feel you are protecting yourself or someone else? Would being open, help you attain peace? Is there a way you could atone for what you did before?

Who did you look up to while growing up?

. . .

WHICH AUTHORITY FIGURE INSPIRED YOU? What were their prevalent qualities?

DO you find those traits in yourself?

IN WHAT WAYS do you feel you can enhance those traits?

IN WHAT WAYS have you been letting yourself down recently, and how can you be better?

WHEN YOU CONSIDER YOUR HEALTH, your family, and your finances, do you feel you've been honest enough to yourself regarding them?

CAN you recall the lies you previously told yourself?

HOW HONEST ARE you to yourself at this moment of your life?

. . .

WHAT IS your last mean thought? Did you express the thought openly? Did the recipient deserve it? Did you feel you were too critical?

THINK of the person who may have let you down the most. Are they still in contact with you? What do you feel about them at this moment?

DO YOU HAVE REGRETS? Rank your worst regrets in life from top to bottom as you can recall them. Will the list be long?

HOW CAN you make peace with your regrets? Consider this. Acknowledge that you did your best.

WHAT'S the worst memory from your childhood that you remember? Do you remember anyone being there for you? Who was this person, and how did he or she comfort you?

WHAT WOULD you like to say to this person right now?

. . .

ARE there situations in your life that you wished had different outcomes? What are they? If things had happened differently, would it have improved your life? How would it have improved your life?

IS your life better since it didn't work out? How is it better? Can you state how?

ARE THERE other traumatic childhood memories you remember or can try to recall?

ARE there character flaws or traits you somehow link to your childhood? What's the worst of these traits? Do you blame anyone for it? Who is this person?

HOW DO you feel about them right now?

. . .

WHAT ARE the worst things you can recall about your parents? Do you possess similar attributes to your parents?

HOW ARE you different from your parents?

OF ALL THE emotions anyone could provoke in you, which is the worst?

WHAT'S your general feeling about your childhood? Do you consider it mostly negative or positive?

WHO MADE you feel mostly safe while growing up, and who always let you down?

HOW DO melodramatic people make you feel? Do you feel you can be dramatic occasionally?

IS THERE a long-standing grudge you have with someone? Why have you struggled to let it go? What do you think you can do to let it go?

. . .

CAN you remember who you once had an argument with or some form of conflict? How did you resolve it? Did you become cautious of the person ever since? How did he or she make you feel?

WHAT'S your biggest concern about any of your relationships currently?

How DO you feel about asking people for help? Do you feel ashamed, worried, or anxious when you do? Does it make you feel weak or inferior? Do you worry that you might be taken advantage of if you ask for help?

WHAT WOULD EASILY MAKE you feel self-conscious?

Do you think you feel unsafe? Why would this be?

. . .

How could your childhood have been better? If something had happened differently, would it have made you feel much better about your childhood?

What could anyone possibly say to you to bring you to your knees? What is it about those words that give them this amount of power? How can you begin to relinquish power from these words?

Is there someone you might have let down the most? What circumstance(s) led to this? Was it out of your control? Does this trouble you? If it does, how do you intend to make peace with the situation?

Would you like to communicate with this person? Write a letter to the person telling them how you've felt since then. It doesn't matter if you decide to send it or not.

What does being *free*, mean to you?

. . .

HAVE you ever considered your purpose? Do you ever feel like you didn't meet your purpose? Do you feel short? What gives you a sense of purpose for all the things you can consider in life?

WHEN YOU THINK of the people close to you, do you feel there are things about them you can change? What could those things be?

HOW CAN you improve your relationship with the people around you?

DO you think you can do better with the way you resolve conflicts?

LOOKING at the tasks you've done so far, have you considered certain things you can improve about yourself?

WHAT DO you value most about yourself?

. . .

WHAT DO the people around you value most about you?

WHAT ARE the things that make you feel self-worth or that make you feel valuable?

WHAT WOULD you want your community, friends, and family to recognize you for?

EXCELLENT WORK SHADOW WORKER, you have successfully made it to the other side. I am so proud of you. I truly hope you find these journaling prompts helpful. I hope you're doing alright. These questions are hard, but they are meant to challenge you, that is what growing is about.

However, now you have the journaling lists, it's time to get a journal for yourself. You could use any book you want, but if you have a journal you like, it's easier to be motivated to do the journaling work. Motivation will also lead to consistency. Find one that's beautiful and contains enough pages for writing.

Head over www.goodselfhealinghabits.com for a list of journals and planners that we have or would recommend as it would save you time and money. I hope you enjoyed this book. If you did, please give us a rating on amazon, hopefully it is a good one . Also share this book with friends and family who you know needs this! Be sure to check out our other reads on shadow work, meditation, journaling, and self-healing practices! We'll, see you very soon.

BEFORE WE PART WAYS

At this point, you've taken a big step to become your full self. You took a proactive step by reading this book to this point because you value growth, because you value being better, and because you've come to acknowledge you needed to walk away from the ordinary and incomplete version of yourself. All the lost pages of yourself are being gathered to form the complete version of you. You're getting to achieving full wholesomeness, and that is one of the things this book aimed to help you achieve.

You learned about who you are. You discovered that your parts are made of two halves, like a coin, and they both matter. You discovered that all this while, you've only been able to show the world and even yourself, the persona part of you – the part that contains the picture of yourself you're more comfortable displaying to yourself and the world. You discovered that your shadow self, that is, the other half, is part of who you are. You had this part of you buried for so long. It haunted you without you even knowing. It pre-determined how you acted, reacted, or behaved in pressure situations. It brought out the worst in you without you even knowing. It did this because you denied it, buried it, and repressed it.

It's not your fault, don't blame yourself for your suffering all these years as a result. My goal was to help you bring out the best of yourself, not to blame yourself, to help you accept responsibility & not be so self-critical. Part of doing that was to also let you know that reaching out to your shadow self was the first step to healing. For the first time, or perhaps not, you realized that you must be in a good relationship with your shadow. You learned that engaging in some shadow mind exercises is necessary to shadow your work journey because it brings you in contact with your lost self. You learned about journaling, for example, and how it plays a huge role in not just getting in contact with your shadow, but integrating her. Isn't that amazing? Yes, you can integrate your shadow and make her part of you. Journaling, and engaging in spiritual exercises such as Tonglen, Vipassana, and Samatha Meditation.

Recall also that your dark side manifests in different forms. It could either manifest as sexual obsession, narcissism, inferiority complex, egotism, self-loath, or as anything at all that seem to stand in the way of you achieving the peace you desire. Because of the denial you've had about the existence of this part of you, you struggled in your relationships, you were less happy, and you often felt incomplete. Now, you've come to realize that continuously denying this part of you wasn't going to make you feel better, but embracing it would. And what this meant is that, acknowledging the part of you that has been there all this while was your brave step to connecting with your shadow.

Your shadow is a result of the childhood traumas you experienced growing up. You weren't the one who put those traumas there. Yes, you may have made some bad decisions, but every one of us made naïve decisions. We made decisions that if we had some experiences then, we would have made wiser choices. But what we couldn't also control was how we were treated as children. We wished our dads were there. We wished our moms understood us better. We wished we weren't bullied. We wished we had the kind of childhood the other kids had. We didn't choose where we were born, our skin color, our ethnicity, or our gender. Nature did. So, we've to accept what we are, and how we've become as a result and love ourselves rather than spite our being. This is what I've tried to teach you here.

Also, remember your inner, lost child. The part of you which your shadow reflects. The girl that used to sit in the corner and mope after another sad day of being bullied or harassed by other boys or girls. The child that didn't understand what parental love felt like, or what it meant to live like a child; that is, to be free, to play, to have fun with friends, to dream, and to aspire to be great. You realized that this child and her memories are hidden in the dark corner of your subconscious, controlling your life because your ego-self has shut her there because of the unpleasant memory bag she shoves at your face. But like a rebellious child, she needs to be understood, loved, embraced and managed. Because if you didn't do this, she'd control you. And the last thing you want is for this to happen. So, you learned that you must be in control. You must take charge and own her, lovingly.

Stay with me as we end. Remember, in your shadow work journey, engaging in spiritual exercises are crucial to healing. You've seen some of the exercises and steps to doing them. Keep practicing, until it becomes part of yourself. We grow by the little steps we take to build our spirit because engaging our pure, untainted spirit is an effective way to lead a peaceful, tranquil life. If you wish to apply the same practices here within your journey to self-discovery and total healing of yourself using Light-Work, look for our book, Awaken Your Zen in stores, and amazon, and we will dive deeper into true; Self-Healing.

When you continue this journey, you'll begin to see some very creative and unique parts of yourself you didn't know existed. Yes. You won't only discover negative or unpleasant parts of yourself. You'll see that shadow work will bring out the flowers that laid behind the shadows you buried.

Now, you have the tools to live a more peaceful and fulfilled life, go ahead, and live your best one.

REFERENCES

Becker, J (2016, January 16) 10 Tips to Start Living in the Present Moment https://www.becomingminimalist.com/10-tips-to-start-living-in-the-present/

Brown, J. Inner child healing: 5 surprisingly powerful exercises https://ideapod.com/5-surprisingly-powerful-ways-to-heal-your-wounded-inner-child/

Dimas, J. (2020, April, 15) SHADOW WORK: 4 STEPS FOR POWERFUL REALIGNING WITH SELF https://jessicadimas.com/shadow-work/

Fosu, K. (2020, November 24) Shadow Work: A Simple Guide to Transcending The Darker Aspects of Yourself https://medium.com/big-self-society/

shadow-work-a-simple-guide-to-transcending-the-darker-aspects-of-the-self-e948ee285723

Fuller K. (2020, June 14). 5 Elements of Shadow Work You Must Incorporate to Become Your Highest Self. https://medium.com/illumination/5-elements-of-shadow-work-you-must-incorporate-to-become-your-highest-self-6f3d35205291

Grey, J. (2019, January 2020) How To Own Your Shadow Before It Owns You. https://www.jordangrayconsulting.com/shadow/

Gupta, S. (2021, August 8) What Is Trauma Therapy? https://www.verywellmind.com/trauma-therapy-definition-types-techniques-and-efficacy-5191413

Hurst, K. How To Use Daily Positive Affirmations With The Law of Attraction https://www.thelawofattraction.com/positive-daily-affirmations/

Lopez, C (n.d.). How to Let Go of the Past for Good. Retrieved August 15, 2021 from https://www.youtube.com/watch?v=tAof_Z5wye0

https://en.m.wikipedia.org/wiki/Shadow_(psychology) retrieved 15th August, 2021.

https://en.m.wikipedia.org/wiki/Unconscious_mind retrieved 15th August, 2021.

Lopez, C (n.d.). Healing the Inner Child: Here's What You Must Do. Retrieved 15 August, 2021. https://www.youtube.com/watch?v=rTnEPNbtJtA

Jacobson S. (2017, September 7th). Your 'Shadow' Self – What It Is, And How It Can Help You https://www.harleytherapy.co.uk/counselling/shadow-self.htm

Jeffrey, S. A Definitive Guide to Jungian Shadow Work: How to Get to Know and Integrate Your Dark Side https://scottjeffrey.com/shadow-work/#What_is_the_Shadow

Jeffrey, S. A Definitive Guide to Jungian Shadow Work: How to Get to Know and Integrate Your Dark Side https://scottjeffrey.com/shadow-work/

Luna, A. (2021, June 12). Shadow Work: The Ultimate Guide https://lonerwolf.com/shadow-work-demons/#h-what-happens-when-you-reject-your-shadow

Morley, C. (2017, July 1) Using dreams to explore the shadow https://www.psychologies.co.uk/using-dreams-explore-shadow

Nichols, S. (2020, May 3rd). Root Chakra Healing: Everything you Need to Know https://onyxintegrative.com/root-chakra-healing/

O'Brien, E. (2021, June 20). The Healing Powers of Yoga Nidra

Owens, L.R. (2021, June 2). How to Practice Shamatha Meditation. https://www.lionsroar.com/how-to-practice-shamatha/

Othon, J. Carl Jung and the Shadow: The Ultimate Guide to the Human Dark Side https://highexistence.com/carl-jung-shadow-guide-unconscious/

Raab, D. (2018 April, 28). Journaling the Sensuous Shadow https://www.google.com/amp/s/www.psychologytoday.com/us/blog/the-empowerment-diary/201804/journaling-the-sensuous-shadow%3famp

Ruiz, A. (2019, September 16) On the True Nature of Intimacy, Shadow Work, and Love https://medium.com/change-your-mind/on-the-true-nature-of-intimacy-shadow-work-and-love-bf79fce69173

Saxe, S. (2021, January 11). 7 Ways to Face Your Shadow Side and Express Your True Self After 60 https://sixtyandme.com/7-ways-to-face-your-shadow-side-and-express-your-true-self-after-60/

Sol, M. (2012, June 12) Shadow Self: How to Embrace Your Inner Darkness (3 Techniques). https://lonerwolf.com/shadow-self/

Sullivan, C. (2021, January 7th). The Benefits of Vipassana Meditation and How to Get Started https://www.healthline.com/health/vipassana-meditation#about-vipassana

Tunstall, K. (2021, March 23) 50 Shadow Work Journal Prompts to Help You Realise Your True

Potential   https://www.refinedprose.com/shadow-work-prompts/#

Ward, R. P. and Ward, L. (2021, May 20) Loving-Kindness: Healing Your Inner Child https://www.lionsroar.com/loving-kindness-healing-your-inner-child/

Chodron, P. Tonglen Instruction

Made in the USA
Monee, IL
20 September 2024